# Cajun

# MEN
## COOK

### Recipes, Stories &
### Food Experiences from
### Louisiana Cajun Country

Beaver Club of Lafayette
Lafayette, Louisiana

Additional copies may be obtained at the cost of $16.95, plus $2.95 postage and handling, each book.

Send To:

Beaver Club of Lafayette
P.O. Box 2744
Lafayette, La. 70502


ISBN: 0-9642486-0-3

First Printing, 10,000 Quantity, October, 1994
Second Printing, 15,000 Quantity, May, 1995


Printed in the USA by

**WIMMER**
The Wimmer Companies, Inc.
Memphis • Dallas

# TABLE OF CONTENTS

# BEAVERS COOK CAJUN—OR VICE-VERSA?

Cuisine is one of the most visible and appealing facets of Cajun culture. Found only in south Louisiana, where generations of French, Indian, Spanish, and Creole cooks have contributed to its development, Cajun cuisine is arguably one of the world's best culinary traditions. Many of the best Cajun cooks are men.

Yes, Cajun men cook! They seldom cook for one or two guests, and they never cook alone. They cook because they love good food, but also because they love the camaraderie, the good times, and the story telling that inevitably accompany meals. Whether preparing blackened redfish on the banks of the bayou or barbecuing a suckling pig on the patio (where cooking time is often gauged by the amount of beer in the cooler), Cajun men have an innate talent for creating taste treats that frequently evolve into legendary culinary delights. Explore the pages and experience the dishes that have made the entire world rave about Cajun cooking.

Bon appétit!

*In putting together the recipes for this cookbook, members of the Beaver Club of Lafayette noted another thing Cajun Men do, besides Cook—they tell jokes (often at their own expense). Nothing is too sacred to poke fun at, including their own intelligence, their way of life, their friends, etc. It's all just a part of the joie de vivre for which Cajuns are so well known!*

# INTRODUCTION

Most people eat to live, but folks in Louisiana's Acadian country live to eat! Few places in this country, indeed in this world, exhibit such a widespread preoccupation with the preparation and consumption of food. This is because cooking and eating are integral components—some would say the most important ingredients—of major Cajun social rituals. Cajun men are among the best practitioners of Acadiana's culinary arts, and some of their best recipes appear within these pages.

Why have we published a men's cookbook when women have traditionally been responsible for food preparation? Why, after centuries of what proved to be a perfectly satisfactory arrangement, are so many men cooking? We are not talking about professional chefs; we are talking about ordinary run-of-the-mill guys—business men, professional men, craftsmen, salesmen, etc. In the twenty-two parish area of south Louisiana called Acadiana, virtually all men cook, and they do it with flair and originality. In fact, Cajuns have elevated cooking to an art form. Many Cajuns are widely recognized as accomplished chefs.

To appreciate how and why this came about, you must first know a little history of our area and its people. The Indians were here first, and they had their own cuisine, based on locally available foods. Then came the Spanish, French, Italians, Africans, native-born free people of color, refugees from Hispañiola, Acadians from Nova Scotia, and "les Américains"—as English-speaking settlers from the East Coast were called—each with their own distinctive cuisine.

The first Acadians had emigrated from France to Acadie (present-day Nova Scotia) in the early 1600s. These French pioneers established themselves as farmers, and they soon prospered, despite frequent invasions and the repeated transfer of the colony between France and Great Britain. Acadie became a permanent British possession in 1713, and the colony's name was changed to Nova Scotia. In 1755, Governor Charles Lawrence of Nova Scotia, acting without necessary royal authorization, ordered the expulsion of the colony's large Acadian population, ostensibly because they refused to renew their oath of allegiance to the British monarch. Some escaped to modern-day New Brunswick, but most were deported to the British colonies along the East

Coast and, later, to France. Many exiled Acadians eventually travelled to south Louisiana, where they attempted to reunite their scattered families.

In Louisiana, the Acadians came into contact with Creoles, Indians, Spaniards, Africans and other groups that they had not previously encountered in their long North American experience. An eminently pragmatic people, the Acadians borrowed survival skills from all of their new neighbors as a means of facilitating their adjustment to their new surroundings. The resulting exchange of culinary techniques, when married to new foods found in Louisiana, gave birth to both Cajun and Creole cuisines.

"Creole" is the French corruption of the Spanish word "criollo," a term meaning native or indigenous to an area. The term eventually came to designate anything born, grown, or developed in the Americas, including people, tomatoes, onions, ponies, and, ultimately, cuisine. The best Creole cooking, found in and around New Orleans and along Bayou Teche, reflects African influences to a greater extent than its Cajun counterpart.

While both Creole and Acadian dishes may begin with a roux (a mixture of oil and flour browned over a low fire) and the "holy trinity" of Cajun cooking, (sautéed celery, onion, and bell pepper) that is where the similarity ends. Cajun cuisine resembles old home style French cooking in that it is hardy, simple, inexpensive, and fresh through the exclusive use of local products. Cajun cooks traditionally utilize black cast iron pots for this style of cooking, known locally as "smothering," but more properly termed braising. Spices and herbs are used to enhance the flavor of the main ingredient but never to overpower it. The seasonings are often combinations of those introduced into Louisiana cooking by the Spanish, French, Indians, and Africans. This accounts for the subtle and often exotic flavors so highly prized by food aficionados. Because of its French and early North American heritage in which meals were prepared in a cauldron suspended over a hearth, Acadian cuisine features many one-dish meals such as gumbos, stews, étouffées, and jambalayas.

Creole cuisine tends to be a more complex blend of French, Spanish, Italian, and African. It employs a variety of cooking styles such as braising, grilling, and sautéing and uses many herbs and seasonings along with frequent use of tomato sauce. In both

6

styles, fresh seafood, wild game, beef, pork, poultry, and a variety of fresh produce make it reasonably easy to produce an exceptionally tasty, and healthy meal. The defining line between the two styles is consequently becoming increasingly blurred as area chefs, both amateur and professional, continue to experiment and broaden their culinary repertoires by including dishes from both culinary traditions.

This evolutionary process reflects the very essence of the Cajun and Creole culinary traditions which has always been adaptability and reliance on local foods. For many years Louisiana vehicle registration plates have borne the legend "Sportman's Paradise." This is no idle boast! Louisiana has duck, quail, dove, geese, deer, squirrel, rabbit, large and small mouth bass, bream, crappie, perch, catfish, alligator, turtle, crab, crawfish, shrimp, oyster, speckled trout, redfish, grouper, drum, flounder, and many others. Many hunters and fishermen naturally maintain camps in the state, and particularly in south Louisiana. Acadian men love hunting and fishing, and, next to the thrill of the catch or the kill, local outdoorsmen prize the joy of preparing and sharing their bounty with friends. Some of the best food we have ever eaten was cooked at Acadiana hunting or fishing camps.

From the time a boy is old enough to hunt or fish he is exposed to men who cook their catch. Cooking and eating are as much a part of this sporting adventure as the actual hunt. Under these circumstances you can begin to appreciate how a boy, who cooks his first fish when he is ten years old and makes his first duck gumbo when he is twelve, gradually improves his cooking skills and eventually looks for new ways to experiment with food preparation. This innovative spirit has led to a great variety of home-made barbecue pits, smokers, Cajun microwaves, and really unusual crawfish boiling rigs. It has also produced some very fine cooks and some most unusual cooking styles. Deep fried turkey, for example, is currently an Acadiana delicacy. A twelve- or fifteen-pound turkey hen is injected with liquid seasoning using a large hypodermic syringe. The bird is then submerged in cooking oil that has been heated to 350 degrees in a black iron pot. The turkey will be cooked to perfection in one hour and the meat will be very tender and moist.

We touched earlier on the pervasive interest Cajuns share in food and its preparation. Acadiana boasts many dining clubs. Clubs are generally composed of five or six couples, and each couple hosts the entire group in their home once a year for an elaborate dinner. At these gatherings, most of the guests usually congregate in the kitchen observing the food preparation while enjoying a glass of wine. Participants also frequently exchange recipes and discuss cooking techniques. This is especially true when the cooking is done by men—whether in the kitchen or at an outdoor grill.

Our own Beaver Club members are no strangers to the grill; they cook and serve 4,000 barbecue chicken dinners at an annual fund raiser.

Now that you have an appreciation of the reasons Cajun men cook, we hope you will use this book as a guide to what they cook and how they make it taste so remarkably good. Bon appétit!

# MAP OF LOUISIANA

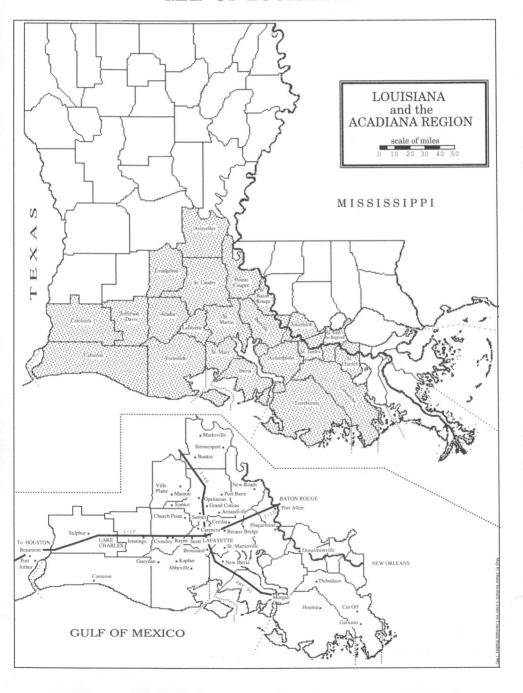

# ACADIANA

Acadiana, a cultural area established by the state legislature on June 2, 1971, includes the parishes of Acadia, Avoyelles, Ascension, Assumption, Calcasieu, Cameron, Evangeline, Iberia, Iberville, Jefferson Davis, Lafayette, Lafourche, Pointe Coupée, St. Charles, St. James, St. John, St. Landry, St. Martin, St. Mary, Terrebonne, Vermilion, and West Baton Rouge. The cultural region was established by the legislature in recognition of the area's uniqueness, grounded upon "the strong French Acadian cultural aspects of said region." Unlike North Louisiana, which is populated primarily by Anglo-American and African-American Protestants, Acadiana is predominantly Catholic, and its ethnically and racially diverse population shares a French-based culture introduced into the region in the late eighteenth century by hundreds of Acadian exiles. Over the past two hundred years, Acadians, Creoles, French Royalists, Bonapartists, and various groups of nineteenth-century French expatriates and their descendants have interacted to produce a cultural amalgam now euphemistically known as Cajun. Persons of German, Hispanic, English, and even African-American heritage as well as more recent immigrants have come to share in the Cajun culture.

Cajun cuisine is a product of this synthetic culture, with every major cultural component contributing to the unique mixture of cooking techniques, spices, and ingredients that has captured the hearts, minds, and palates of the culinary world. In this culinary tradition, there are as many styles of food preparation as there are individual cooks and, in Acadiana, everyone is an excellent cook. But, of course, men and women, generally tend to cook differently, and in different venues. The recipes set out within constitute the best introduction to the way men cook in Acadiana.

# THE BEAVER CLUB

The Lafayette Lions Club, "mother club" of the current Beaver organization, was established on December 13, 1939, and chartered by Lions International in January 1940. Charter members included a substantial number of leading local businessmen, lawyers, and elected officials who had not been moved to join other, more traditional civic clubs. Fundraising during the World War II era was on a modest scale and directed primarily toward the Lions Club eyeglass and children's assistance programs, but, shortly after World War II, the Lions Club took a momentous step which would transform it into Lafayette's premier civic organization. In the 1930s, the Girard family had donated to the City of Lafayette a large wooded tract adjacent to Southwestern Louisiana Institute (present-day University of Southwestern Louisiana). Though the donation stipulated that the tract was to be developed as a park or that ownership would revert to the Girard family, the city was unable to undertake the project because World War II had effectively removed the necessary money and manpower from the community. In October 1946, the Lions Club entered into a five-year contract with the city to raise funds for clearing the property and developing it into Lafayette's first major park. The city trustees approved the proposal, and the ambitious park project was underway!

A single truck for removing felled trees constituted the only power equipment utilized by the club in the early stages of the park's development. Almost all the clearing was done by hand with axes and crosscut saws. Most Saturdays were "work days" with the members and their families turning out en masse. One report indicates that the position of one member as a beer company representative kept the project going! By 1951 the major work had been completed. The club constructed the park lake in 1952 and added an open air amphitheater the following year. The Lions Club funded these improvements by staging an annual minstrel show. Talent in the group was exceptional, and most shows were sellouts. During the mid-1950s, the Lions used a radio auction for fundraising, designating most of the proceeds to park improvements, the eyeglass program, and the wheelchair fund.

In 1959, the Club was notified that a group of men had approached the Lions International to charter a second Southside

Lafayette Lions Club. The officers of the existing club pleaded with the International officials to deny the request noting that it could only lead to confusion in fundraising, and that the "hands-on" approach to park improvements required as much manpower as could be mustered. When the Lions International authorized a second Lafayette chapter, the Hub City's original Lions group surrendered its charter and became an independent organization. By mid-1959, the group had reorganized as the "Beaver Club," the name symbolizing the club's eager-beaver involvement in parks.

As the club made itself over, it also changed its approach to fundraising, moving its auction from radio to television. The generosity of local merchants, who donated merchandise for the auction, and the new television format proved a most successful combination.

The success of their first TV fundraiser led the Beavers to undertake their first major project as an independent club. The airport grounds in 1960 included a low, heavily wooded area along the Vermilion River. The Beaver Club proposed to transform this area into another major city park, and, with approval of the city administration, the organization did just that! Playground equipment, picnic areas, baseball diamonds, tennis courts, a fishing lake, and a boat launch site transformed this once abandoned area into a citywide recreational center.

* * *

The improbable, irreverent, irrepressible Beaver Club! No dry recounting of their history really captures the spirit and the camaraderie that are the basis of their existence. Despite premature predictions of an early demise, the club became a dynamic, one-of-a-kind organization. Club presidents have consistently struggled to maintain some semblance of decorum in meetings that are often characterized by verbal barbs and bombshells, sometimes ribald humor, and an enduring conviction that meeting should be fun—and sometimes even enlightening. After thirty-three years, the Beavers are still intent on keeping alive the treasured tradition of service to the community—while "passing a good time"!

# NON-MEMBERS WHO CONTRIBUTED RECIPES

Danny Abel
Francis Arceneaux
Robert M. Arceneaux
Joel P. Babineaux
Allen R. Bares
John Berthelot
J. Rayburn Bertrand
David Billeaud
Robert Billeaud, Sr.
Robert Earl Billeaud
Dale A. Boudreaux
Jack Bright
Arthur Carlin
Allen Chiquelin
Peter Cloutier
Lloyd Comeaux
William Courville
John Daigre
Robert Darnall
John Doucet
David Fisher
Lee Fontenot
Bernard Francka
Stephen Gauthier
Mike Hamsa

Sterling Hebert
Wayne Hebert
Robert M. Kallam
Dr. Henry Koke
Ewing C. Latimer
Pat Lemoine
Tony Lemoine
Norwood Meiners
Bill Monks
John Montesanto
Irving Pratt
Donald L. Robertson
James Rogers
M. E. Rowe
Randall Rosser
Allen St. Martin
Roy Simoneaud
Wayne Simoneaud
V. P. Simoneaud
Dr. Sweeney Smith
Stanley Trotter
Philip Trahan
Ed Villien
G. M. Vincent
Mike Witkovski
Jeff Zeigner

# BEAVER MEMBERS

Glynn Abel
Max Baer
Don Bacque
Paul Barefield
Brian Barnes
George Berry
Bernard Billeaud
George Billeaud
Boyd Boudreaux
Charles Boudreaux, Jr.
Donald Breaux
Charles Brandt
Bill Busch
Steve Butaud
David Caillier
Bryan Caillier
Gene Cella
Thomas Chance
Richard Chappuis
Chris Christensen
Larry Comeaux
Mark Comeaux
Charles Compton
Art Courville
Joseph Damario
Clay Darnall
Gerry Delaney
Ken Dixon
Ed Doyal
Mark Dubroc
Hubert Dumesnil
James Farley
Lindsey Fisher
Patrick Gaubert
Ronald Gauthier
Buddy Guirovich
Rodney Hamilton
Chuck Hamsa
Thomas Hightower
Thomas Hingle

Scott Hollier
Mario Holloway
Patrick Huval
Mervin Jankower
Steven Jankower
David Koke
David Koke, Jr.
Thomas Kreamer
Roger Larivee
Jack Lavigne
Paul Lemaire
Louis Mann
Randall Mann
Russell Mann
John Melancon
Jack McCabe
Rick Michot
James Miller
Charles Mouton
John Mouton
Robert Mouton
Fritz Muller
Shawn O'Neill
Bill Patton
Wayne Prejean
Steve Rainey
Larry Richard
Russell Richard
Edward Roberson
Thomas Rogers
Edwin Roy
Vincent Saitta
Larry Sides
Ben Skerrett
Jerrel Sonnier
Craig Strait
Vernon Ventress
Jim Vildibill
Larry Whitmeyer

# FATHER COULDN'T MAKE GOOD CHERRY BOUNCE

Our home was built on piers, with the floor two feet above the ground. My older brother and I were already past the "playing with dirt" stage, when, one hot summer afternoon, T'Paul, our youngest brother emerged from the cool ground under the house with a large sealed crock. He had found it when he was digging dirt to make a dam. We sternly admonished T'Paul to do his digging in the opposite corner and to tell no one about his discovery, because we knew that he had found Father's cache of cherry bounce. Father had said that he was going to try Grandfather's recipe because he remembered how good it was. We carefully placed the crock back into its hole about sixteen inches below ground level, filled the hole, and used freshly cut azalea branches to brush away any traces of digging.

That summer, Mother was pleased that we spent so much time with our little brother, even to the extent of digging dams under the house with T-Paul. Yet, we carefully avoided the corner where the treasure was hidden. We wanted to sample Father's cherry bounce, but the crock could not be removed from its hiding place. We devised a plan of connecting straws to reach the crock. The end of the interconnected reed straws fit nicely into a small hole that we made in the seal.

We devised a plan to maintain the amount of liquid in the crock. We simply filled our mouths with water and blew the water into the crock. This procedure worked well until we began to notice that the liquid has lost its "bounce," so we removed the straws, re-sealed the small hole, and covered our tracks.

Fall came, and Father wanted to be a part of the neighbors' daughter's wedding. He invited the neighbors for dinner, and, after dinner, he announced to the older men that he had something

**15**

special outside. He proudly unearthed the crock, and, in the darkness, he proudly broke the seal. Using a dipper, he filled everyone's glasses. But something was wrong; the cherry bounce certainly did not taste like the one Grandfather made. Quickly dumping the mixture out of the crock, he led the group back into the house for coffee, muttering "Some days chicken, some days feathers!"

Years later, when Father finally gave us Grandfather's recipe for cherry bounce, he remarked, "I tried it once, but it didn't turn out." We did not have the heart to tell him how well he had succeeded! See recipe on page 19.

# Cajun

## MEN COOK
## APPETIZERS, BEVERAGES, & BREADS

# APPETIZERS, BEVERAGES AND BREADS

# CHERRY BOUNCE

nutmeg
cloves
fresh or canned berries or
   fruit

sugar

In a wide-mouth container place layers of nutmeg, cloves and fresh or canned berries or fruit between sugar layers until about 2 inches from the top. Add your favorite liquor until the mixture is completely covered. Cover and cap. Let stand three or more months. Add liquor as you use the mixture.

*Many enjoy the resulting liquor as a sauce for ice cream. Some have felt that there is a taste of cinnamon. Cherry Bounce was at one time a very common liquor throughout the southeastern United States.*

# CRAWFISH DIP

1 stick oleo
2 pounds cleaned chopped
   crawfish
1 cup green onions

1 16 ounce package cream
   cheese
hot sauce, salt, pepper,
   parsley and onion tops

Melt oleo. Sauté crawfish and green onions for 10 minutes. Melt cream cheese into crawfish and cook until bubbly. Add other seasoning. Serve in chafing dish with melba rounds.

# SEAFOOD COCKTAIL DIP

½ cup catsup
2 tablespoons fresh lemon
   juice
½ tablespoon
   Worcestershire sauce

⅛ teaspoon pepper sauce
¼ teaspoon horseradish
⅛ teaspoon garlic powder

Blend well all ingredients. For best results, put in refrigerator at least one hour before serving. This is a standard dip used in Cajun country for crawfish, shrimp and crab boils. It is also used as a dipping sauce to eat with raw oysters. It is easy to make and keeps well in the refrigerator.

# JOHN'S CRAB DIP SUPREME

1½ sticks margarine
2 large onions, chopped
2 stalks celery with tops, chopped
3 tablespoons parsley, chopped
3 pounds fresh or frozen crabmeat, or (seven 6½ ounce cans crabmeat)
1 large can evaporated milk
2 pounds soft processed cheese, cut in small pieces

1 10½ ounce can mushroom soup
½ teaspoon garlic powder
½ teaspoon thyme
1 teaspoon browning and seasoning sauce (optional if you want tan rather than white colored dip)
bread crumbs (to thicken)
salt and pepper to taste

Melt margarine in black iron pot. Add onions and celery. Cook with lid on low fire for 20 minutes. Stir as needed. Add parsley, crabmeat, cheese, garlic powder, mushroom soup, thyme and browning and seasoning sauce (optional). Cook on low heat with lid for one hour. Stir as needed. Add salt and pepper to taste. Thicken as desired with bread crumbs. Simmer 15 minutes. Keep warm when serving. Can be frozen. Melba rounds are ideal to use with this dish.

*Cook time: 1¾ hour*                    *¾ gallon*

**This is a 4-star recipe which has been copied hundreds of times—but never duplicated. "Close Enough" is reward in itself.**

# ARTICHOKE HEARTS DIP

2 or 3 6 ounce cans chopped ripe olives
2 teaspoons onion (or about ¼ to ½ onion)
1½ cups sharp cheddar cheese, grated
½ cup or more mayonnaise

1 or 2 jars marinated artichoke hearts, not drained
Cilantro or parsley to taste
Red pepper or jalapeño pepper to taste

Chop olives and onion. Stir in the grated cheese. Add mayonnaise, artichoke hearts and seasonings. Broil in oven until bubbly if used as a spread, on English muffins or bake at 350°F or so until bubbly and serve with tortilla chips.

## ARTICHOKE DIP

2 cans drained artichoke hearts
1 cup mayonnaise

1 package Italian dressing mix (dry)
1 can olives, drained

Chop artichoke hearts and olives. Mix all ingredients and chill. Serve with crackers.

Easy and delicious.

## CHILI RELLENO DIP

2 large tomatoes, peeled and chopped
1 4 ounce can green chilies
1 4 ounce can black olives, chopped

4 shallots, with tops, chopped fine
3 tablespoons olive oil
1½ teaspoons garlic salt
salt and pepper to taste

Mix all ingredients well. Refrigerate for a few hours. Serve with tortilla chips.

*3 cups*

*This is a dish easy to fix and can be prepared a few days in advance. Keeps well in refrigerator.*

This dish is excellent as an ingredient of Spanish Omelet.

## SPICY QUESO DIP

1 pound ground chuck beef
1 pound spicy sausage
1 can undiluted Cream of Mushroom Soup
2 cups hot salsa
1 pound pasteurized process cheese spread

1 pound aged cheddar cheese, diced into 1 inch cubes
deep-fried tortilla wedges or nacho chips

In a large, heavy-bottomed skillet, brown beef and sausage meat over medium heat. Drain fat from pan and discard; drain in a fine colander for a good while. Add mushroom soup and salsa, stirring to mix well. Turn heat to low and add cubed cheeses. Cook, stirring constantly until cheese melts.

*½ gallon*

## ALLEN'S CAJUN SALSA

1 16 ounce can Mexican
  tomatoes
1 medium onion, peeled
  and quartered

½ lime, juice only
3 jalapeños, seeded
¼ cup Cilantro, minced

Blend all ingredients well; serve with chips and beans.

*1 pint*

## SHRIMP SPREAD

1 8 ounce package cream
  cheese (softened)
2 pounds boiled shrimp,
  chopped fine
1 lemon, juice only
5 green onion tops, minced

mayonnaise to soften
hot sauce to taste
1 tablespoon Worcestershire
  sauce
salt and pepper to taste

Soften cream cheese, add lemon juice, shrimp, onion tops and mayonnaise to spreading consistency. Stir in seasonings (salt, hot sauce and pepper to taste). Serve with crackers. Keep refrigerated. Better if made one day ahead of time.

*Yields 2 cups*

## SHRIMP MOLD

1 can tomato soup
1 envelope plain gelatin
1 8 ounce package cream
  cheese (softened)
1 cup mayonnaise
¼ cup chopped green
  onions

½ cup chopped celery
2 cans broken shrimp (or 2
  cups of chopped, peeled,
  cooked shrimp)
salt, hot sauce and red
  pepper to taste
¼ cup boiling water

Sprinkle gelatin over boiling water in double boiler and dissolve. Add softened cream cheese; fold into liquid until blended. Add other ingredients and pour into a 1½ quart mold, then refrigerate until firm.

## TORTILLA ROLL-UPS

1 8 ounce package cream
  cheese
¾ bunch chopped green
  onions

1 heaping tablespoon
  seasoning
1 package 10 large tortillas

Mix first 3 ingredients in mixing bowl. Spread with rubber spatula onto tortilla (spread about 1 large spoonful on each). Slice into bite-size pieces. Serve with salsa as a dip.

*Yields 4 dozen.*

## BILL STONECIPHER'S TEXAS TRASH

1 medium box each
  Cheerios, Rice Chex, Corn
  Chex, Wheat Chex, cheese
  crackers and pretzels
2 large cans mixed nuts

1 12 ounce jar dry roasted
  peanuts
2 12 ounce bags pecans
  (shelled) or more if desired

Mix together in turkey roaster or large pans. Heat oven at 275°F. In a pot on top of the stove, heat:

3 sticks oleo
1 cup bacon, ham or
  sausage drippings (not too
  dark)

3 tablespoons garlic salt,
  onion salt and hot sauce
2 tablespoons
  Worcestershire sauce

Pour liquid and spices over dry ingredients stirring constantly, but keep ¼ of liquid to stir into dry mix at 15 minute intervals. Bake uncovered 1 hour, stirring and adding liquid every 15 minutes. Allow to cool and store in containers.

## HOT CHEESE DELIGHTS

½ pound sharp cheese,
  grated
½ pound butter

salt, red pepper, and hot
  sauce to taste
2 cups chopped pecans
2 cups sifted flour

Soften butter to room temperature and mix with grated cheese; add flour, pecans and seasonings until zesty and spicy. Divide this dough into 3 equal portions. Roll out each portion on a sheet of wax paper and form a long roll about an inch thick. Wrap each of the 3 rolls separately. Put them in foil and freeze until needed. When needed, just slice ½ inch slices and bake in 350°F oven for 15-17 minutes. Only the bottoms should be brown. These are great served warm from the oven but still are good even when cold the next day.

*3 large rolls*

## DON'S ULTIMATE NACHOS

2 pounds ground beef
2 tablespoons vegetable oil
1 large onion, chopped fine
2 large bell peppers,
  chopped fine
4 cloves garlic, minced
sour cream (optional)
1 jar picante sauce
1 2 ounce package taco
  seasoning mix
1 teaspoon sugar

1½ teaspoon salt
½ teaspoon black pepper
⅛ teaspoon cayenne red
  pepper
1 pound Mozzarella cheese
1 8 ounce package jalapeño
  pasteurized process
  cheese spread
1 bunch green onions with
  tops, chopped fine
2 large boxes nacho chips

Heat oil and brown meat in a 4 quart iron pot, about 10 minutes. Add taco seasoning. Simmer, covered for 15 minutes. Add onion, bell pepper, garlic, picante sauce, salt, red and black pepper and sugar. Simmer on low fire, covered 1 hour. Stir as needed. In a 13x9x2 inch baking pan alternate layers of nacho chips, meat, and cheese ending up with cheese on top. Bake in oven at 400°F for 20 minutes until cheese melts. Top with sour cream mix.

*15 servings*

# PIZZA NIBBLES

1 pound fresh loose pork
  sausage
1 pound ground beef
½ teaspoon black pepper
¼ teaspoon thyme
¼ teaspoon tarragon
1 teaspoon salt

2 tablespoons oregano
½ teaspoon garlic salt
½ teaspoon Worcestershire
  sauce
1 pound cheese, grated
2 loaves rye bread, cut into
  triangles

Mix meats and brown in a skillet on medium heat. Drain. Add all other ingredients and cook on low fire until cheese melts. Remove from fire and spread on surfaces of rye bread triangles. Place on a cookie sheet, cover with plastic wrap and place in refrigerator or freezer. When frozen, store in reclosable bags in freezer for future use. Thaw out when needed. If serving soon, remove from refrigerator and then bake in oven at 400°F for 10 minutes.

*100 triangles*

*You will find this a party stealer appetizer. Very economical to fix for parties, wedding receptions etc. It can be fixed weeks ahead of time, and then stored for future use.*

This is a very appropriate appetizer for an Italian theme dinner party.

# OYSTERS ON THE LAKE

raw oysters to fill a tin pie
  plate

4 strips bacon cooked,
  drained, crumbled
4 ounces Parmesan cheese

Cocktail Sauce:
1 ounce horseradish
6 ounces Catsup

½ teaspoon Worcestershire
  sauce
½ teaspoon lemon juice

These may be cooked on any type of B.B.Q. pit with a cover. Fill bottom of pie plate with oysters and oyster water. Cover with cocktail sauce, sprinkle with bacon and cheese. Close lid. Check 5 minutes for oysters to curl. When curled, remove and eat.

# CAFÉ AU LAIT

**For 4:**
3 tablespoons sugar          2 cups strong black coffee
2 cups hot milk

**For 10:**
9½ tablespoons sugar          5 cups strong black coffee
5 cups hot milk

Caramelize sugar in iron skillet or pot on medium fire (approximately 10 minutes). Add room temperature milk, stirring to blend in sugar. Slowly bring to boil, stirring to prevent sticking. When it boils, reduce to simmer. While the milk is heating, make French drip coffee. (Okay to substitute, but this method is by far the best!) French drip by setting a drip coffee pot in a pan of water. Keep water in the pan simmering. Putting grounds in place, take simmering water from the pot and slowly pour over grounds. (No more than 3 tablespoons dripped before more is added). All the while, the dripped coffee is sitting in the simmering water. When coffee is made, pour as per recipe amount and adjust sugar. This coffee is an excellent beverage for breakfast!

*4 or 10 cups*

# MILK PUNCH

½ fifth Bourbon          2 half gallons milk (ease of
1 cup White Crème de          storage)
  Menthe          1 pint Half and Half
1 cup Crème de Cocoa          nutmeg for garnish
1½ cups Bar Simple Syrup*

Mix all ingredients. Serve with nutmeg. Can be frozen.

***To make simple syrup, bring to boil 3 cups of water and 1½ cups of sugar.***

## FAMOUS ARTILLERY PUNCH

6 ounces lemon juice
1 tablespoon bitters
½ fifth burgundy or claret
½ fifth dry sherry
½ fifth brandy

1 fifth bourbon
1 fifth champagne
¾ cup sugar (or sweeten to taste)

Mix together above ingredients.

*At one time this recipe was attributed to Retired Colonel Jim Andres of Vernon Parish, Louisiana. The punch is most pleasant and packs a heck of a wallop.*

## CORN MEAL WINE

3 cups corn meal
3 pounds white and brown sugar
1 cake or pack baker's yeast

1 lemon
1 handful of raisins (optional)

Mix corn meal, brown and white sugar, yeast and quartered lemon in a one gallon container. Be sure that the mixture is not hot as it will kill the yeast. If you are using a gallon glass jug, you can simply attach a new balloon to the jug's top. A small pinhole in the balloon will allow the carbon dioxide gas to escape without too much air getting into contact with the mixture. When the balloon deflates, the mixture is finished. Carefully decant into regular size bottles, taking care not to disturb the heavier mixture at the jug's bottom. Or you can syphon the mixture into the bottles. Cap the bottles and set them aside as long as you can stand not touching them. You can now add more mixture to the jug (without yeast) to start again. When the mixture is first started, you can put in a handful of raisins that will eventually add body to the wine. If you are looking for a stronger wine, you can also add a tablespoon of sour milk (which is lactic acid) as this will cause the yeast to work harder to produce alcohol and carbon dioxide.

*An alternative to this recipe is to use rice in place of corn meal. But it is recommended that raisins be used as that definitely adds body and a gallon color to the wine.*

## LLOYD COMEAUX BLOODY MARY

1 46 ounce can tomato
  juice
½ pint vodka
4 good squirts hot sauce,
  more if desired
1½ heaping teaspoon celery
  salt

2 tablespoons
  Worcestershire sauce
1 teaspoon rose lime juice
1 teaspoon horseradish
  (optional)
basil leaves to suit taste
  (optional)

Mix all ingredients in a gallon glass jar, cork or cap, and refrigerate until used.

*8 drinks*

*A gallon jug is ideal for mixing and serving this drink. Serve with fresh lime slices and a stick of celery. Each individual glass served can be self adjusted to individual taste buds with exception of tomato juice.*

## CAJUN COCO-MIX

1 pound chocolate drink
  mix
1 6 ounce jar non-dairy
  creamer

1 box instant dry milk (8
  quart size)
1 cup powdered milk

Mix all ingredients well. Pour ½ cup mixture into mug. Add 1 cup boiling water and mix.

# CORN BREAD AND COUCHE-COUCHE

The portion of Acadiana west of the Atchafalaya River—unlike the area east of the river—traditionally did not produce wheat bread, hence the paucity of bread recipes in this collection. From the time of the Acadian arrival in the late eighteenth century until the 1920s, corn was the staple of the western Cajun diet. *Couche-couche*—corn meal fried in shortening—was the traditional breakfast dish in Cajun households along the western bayous and prairies. The dry, crisp bits of corn batter produced by constantly stirring the corn batter in a black, cast-iron frying pan were eaten—like modern breakfast cereals—with milk, fresh fruit, or preserves. At noon and at supper, hungry Cajuns ate cornbread prepared in open hearths and in Dutch ovens, along with salted meat or wild game and seasonal vegetables. Since the 1920s, rice and, to a lesser extent, white bread have gradually supplanted corn, and corn meal, as the foundation of the Cajun diet.

# BANANA NUT BREAD-MAMA'S RECIPE

**Sift before measuring:**
2 cups flour
½ teaspoon baking powder
½ teaspoon baking soda

¼ teaspoon salt
1 teaspoon cinnamon

**Cream until light:**
¾ cup sugar

¼ cup butter or margarine, softened

**Stir in:**
1 egg
1 cup mashed bananas (3 medium) (Squeeze a few drops of lemon juice on the bananas before adding to the mixture)

¼ teaspoon vanilla extract
3 teaspoons sour milk (put a few drops of vinegar in milk and let stand 10 minutes)
½ cup pecans

Mix together, place in a greased and floured bread pan. Bake at 350°F for one hour.

## PAIN PERDU (LOST BREAD)

3 eggs
¾ cup milk
¼ teaspoon nutmeg
¼ teaspoon vanilla

3 tablespoons butter
8 slices bread (bread of
choice: diet or plain
white)

Heat oven to 250°F. Beat eggs, milk, nutmeg and vanilla. In a large frying pan, melt 1½ tablespoons of butter over medium high heat. Dip half of the bread slices in the egg mixture (both sides and let the excess drip off). Fry the bread in hot butter until golden-brown on both sides, about 5 minutes. Put into heat proof platter and put into the oven to keep warm. Melt the remaining 1½ tablespoons of butter in the pan and dip and fry the remaining bread.

*8 servings*

## PAIN PERDU (LOST BREAD)

3 large eggs, beaten
2 cups milk
4 tablespoons vanilla
extract

4 tablespoons sugar
4 tablespoons brown sugar
12 slices bread

Mix beaten eggs and vanilla. Mix one cup of milk and sugar. Add remaining milk and brown sugar. Mix well. Add to egg mixture and blend well. Use a fork to dip a slice of bread at a time in the batter. Fry on low heat in melted butter. Sprinkle with powdered sugar and serve with honey, preserves, or cane syrup.

*Cook time: 3 minutes*      *Serves 4*      *Pan: Skillet*

*How about the Harvard graduate who thought he'd stump the poor Cajun with his question:*

> *"'Cajun, I'll bet you $25 that you cannot tell me how many seconds there are in a year,' challenged the Harvard graduate. 'Mais dat's a bet I'll take,' said the Cajun. 'Da ansah is 12 seconds in a year.' The Harvard graduate looked puzzled. 'How did you come up with that figure?' the grad asked. As the Cajun held up his hand and started to count on his fingers, he said, 'Dat's easy, cher! Mais look...dere's January 2nd, February 2nd, March 2nd, April...'"*

## SAUSAGE BREAD

1 package (3 loaves)
Bridgeford bread
1 pound pork breakfast
sausage, browned &
drained
1 pound Frey smoked
sausage, browned &
drained

1 pound Mozzarella cheese
1 pound cheddar cheese
1 medium can Parmesan
cheese
1 10½ ounce jar chopped
green olives
2 bunches green onions

Let bread thaw and rise. Roll out thin on a large, flat area; butter dough. Sprinkle equal amounts of ingredients on all three loaves. Tuck sides in jelly-roll fashion. Bake at 375°F for 30-40 minutes.

*Yields 3 loaves*

**May be frozen in foil.**

## MEXICAN CORNBREAD

1 cup yellow cornmeal
¼ cup tasso, (smoked pork
meat), optional
2 eggs, well beaten
¾ cup milk
½ teaspoon soda added to
milk
½ teaspoon salt
¼ teaspoon chili powder

1 16 ounce can yellow
cream corn
1 cup cheddar cheese,
grated
½ cup bacon drippings
2 jalapeño peppers, minced
1 tablespoon canned
pimentos, minced

Mix all ingredients and bake in a greased iron skillet at 350°F for 40 minutes.

*6 servings*

**You will find this recipe quite good, and it is compatible with most dishes which call for chili powder or cumin.**

**Add 1 pound of crawfish tails to the ingredients during preparation of this recipe. You are in for the treat of your life.**

## APACHE BREAD

1 9 inch sour dough bread
16 ounce sharp cheddar
cheese
1 ounce package cream
cheese, softened
1 ounce sour cream
1 stalk green onions,
chopped

1½ teaspoon Worcestershire
sauce
2 cans green chopped
chilies (do not drain)
1 cup chopped boiled ham
1 can chopped black olives

Cut off top of bread and hollow out the inside of the bread. Keep the top intact for replacement in step 3. Combine ingredients and mix well into bowl. Place mixture into bread and replace the top. Place bread on cookie sheet. Bake 1 hour and 15 minutes at 350°F.

## BEER BREAD

3 cups self-rising flour
2½ to 3 tablespoons sugar

1 can beer at room
temperature

Mix ingredients, allowing beer to foam when pouring into the mixture. Put mixture into a greased pan, using greased hands to pat down mixture. Make a deep trench down the center or it will rise too high in the center and crack. Bake in a preheated oven at 375°F for 1 hour. Brush with butter. The crust will be hard and crusty. It will soften as it cools.

**If you have plain flour, you can make self-rising flour by using the following ingredients for 1 cup of self-rising flour:**

1 cup flour
1¼ teaspoon baking powder

⅛ teaspoon salt

*6 servings*

*You can store the bread in a plastic bag in the refrigerator, but it is best to eat the bread the day you bake it. After a few days the beer will cause the bread to turn bitter or sour.*

## SPINACH BREAD SPREAD

1 loaf French bread, split
  lengthwise
4 ounces sharp cheddar
  cheese

4 ounces roll garlic cheese
½ stick butter
1 package frozen spinach,
  defrosted, finely chopped

Mix all ingredients together and spread over inside side of bread. Place in oven face up on a cookie sheet and bake for 10 minutes at 400°F.

*24 pieces*

**Excellent served with soups and salads.**

## BILL AND BONNIE'S CAMPFIRE BISCUITS

2 cups all purpose flour
1 teaspoon salt
1½ tablespoon baking
  powder

¼ cup shortening,
  preferably butter (Mott's
  unsweetened applesauce
  can be used for those
  desirous of less fat in
  their diet)
1 small can evaporated milk
1 small can water

Cut shortening, flour, baking powder and salt together. Make a small crater in the mixture and then add the evaporated milk and water. Mix together with a fork until the mixture globs on the fork. Flour hands as well as any board that you will be using. You can use the empty evaporated milk can to press out biscuit forms. Bake in any type of oven at 450°F for eight to ten minutes. If you use a Dutch oven, each fired charcoal briquette will give off approximately 40°F of heat. Use an uneven number of briquettes, with more on the top than on the bottom. For example, 7 fired briquettes on the top and 6 on the bottom will yield a combined temperature of some 520°F, more than enough to do the job. Using an inverted pie tin in the bottom of the Dutch oven will help to elevate the biscuits from being burned on the bottom.

# GUMBO AT THE RAYNE DROP SALOON, 1886

From the Rayne Signal, March 20, 1886: "The gumbo soiree at the Rayne Drop Saloon last Saturday night was a very enjoyable affair. In addition to the gumbo and palatable beverages served up, amusements of different kinds were indulged in by many present. The music, by the Rayne Mutual Band, was excellent, and added much pleasure to the occasion. Mr. D. Pucheu, the manager of the saloon, displayed good taste in the artistic manner in which he had everything arranged and served out, and with his courtesy and urbanity made all present feel comfortable and at home. Such reunions of gentlemen, when properly conducted, certainly can not be out of place."

# MEN COOK

## GUMBOS, SOUPS, & SALADS

# GUMBOS, SOUPS, SALADS AND SALAD DRESSINGS

# ROUX

Many traditional Cajun recipes begin with the following instruction: "first you make a roux." Roux, made by browning roughly equal portions of flour and oil in a skillet (ideally of cast-iron) over low heat, is used as the base for dishes requiring thick brown gravies—such as fricassees and stews—and gumbos.

Roux is a vestige of Acadiana's French culinary tradition. Prior to the advent of the Dutch oven, cooks throughout the western world used the open hearth method of cooking. In this method, dishes were prepared in cauldrons suspended over hearthfires. As a result, soups, fricassees, stews, and other one-pot dishes were the norm. French cooks routinely used roux as a base for thickening gravies.

French rouxs, however, differ significantly from their Louisiana cousin. French cooks use butter to prepare rouxs that are generally of lighter color (white to light brown) and consistency than those produced in Louisiana kitchens; Louisiana rouxs, on the other hand, are of heavy consistency and are usually from medium to dark brown.

# ROUX

**⅔ cup flour**                **¾ cup salad oil**

In a heavy pot mix the flour and the oil thoroughly before turning on the fire under the pot. After it is mixed, turn the fire on medium to low, stirring constantly. Stir all over the bottom of the pot to be sure that no particles stick to the bottom. As you stir, the roux browns slowly. Do not cook roux fast, because as it reaches the done point, it will be too hot and burn. When your roux is a rich dark brown, cut off fire immediately, while continuing to stir. Add water to lower the temperature slightly so the roux will stop browning. You can also add chopped onions to lower the temperature. Either way, continue to stir until the temperature is lowered sufficiently. Then you may turn your fire on again under the pot and add the rest of the ingredients for your stew or gumbo slowly.

*The measurements above make a roux large enough for a stew with 1 hen, or a gumbo with two pounds of shrimp. If you wish to make a larger recipe, enlarge the recipe in the same proportions given.*

**Roux is the base for stews, gumbos and sauce piquants.**

# ROUX (MICROWAVE)

**1 cup flour**                **2 stalks celery**
**1 large bell pepper**        **3 cups onion**
**1 cup cooking oil**

In one quart microwave safe measuring cup with handle, blend flour and cooking oil until well mixed and no lumps are found. Cook in microwave on high for five minutes, stopping occasionally to stir ingredients with wooden spoon. After five minutes, reset microwave for another five minutes and stop, stir thoroughly to bottom, and restart microwave every thirty seconds. When golden brown, remove from microwave and add chopped vegetables and blend into hot roux, very carefully. Roux will burn skin more than hot grease. To mixed ingredients add boiling water in pot slowly pouring and mixing to lower temperature of roux.

*6 servings*

# ELLENDER'S SEAFOOD GUMBO

5 tablespoons fat (vegetable oil or bacon fat)
1 tablespoon flour, rounded
2 pounds onions, chopped fine
3 stalks celery, chopped fine
1 medium bell pepper, chopped fine
3 pods of garlic, chopped fine
1 lemon (grated rind, remove white pulpy membrane and chop rest of lemon)
a few dashes Worcestershire sauce, hot sauce, thyme, Creole seasoning
2 bay leaves
salt to taste

To the fat add flour and brown, stirring constantly to make scorchy-tasting roux. Add onions, fry slowly until well-browned and reduced to a pulp. Add rest of ingredients at one time and simmer for 30 to 45 minutes.

**Basic Sauce:**
2½ pounds okra
3 pounds fresh shrimp tails, peeled and deveined
1 pound crabmeat
1 pint oysters, onion tops and parsley, handful of each

After cutting in small pieces, cook the okra slowly in a small pot in about 2 tablespoons of fat until no longer ropy, stirring often to prevent scorching or browning. Add to basic sauce and continue to cook for not less than 20 minutes. Add shrimp and crabmeat, and about 10 minutes later, the oysters. Add water to make the sauce of a soupy consistency. Cook for about 20 minutes after the mixture has started to boil. About 10 minutes before serving, add a handful of chopped onion tops and parsley. Serve over rice in soup bowls.

*8 servings*

# SEAFOOD GUMBO

½ cup roux
2 quarts boiling water
1 pound small shrimp
1 pint oysters
1 pound crabmeat
3 cups onion
1 large bell pepper
2 stalks celery

1 tablespoon red pepper
1 teaspoon filé powder
1 tablespoon salt
2 tablespoons parsley
1 tablespoon white pepper
 (or black)
2 tablespoons green onions

Make light to medium colored roux (See Roux directions). Add to large deep pot of boiling water until blended. Add finely chopped onions, bell pepper and celery. Cook on high heat for 30 minutes or until vegetables are tender. Add cleaned small shrimp and cook for two minutes on low heat, add crabmeat and oysters and turn off burner or remove from stove. Season with salt and pepper to taste. Gumbo filé can be added to pot or to individual bowls once served along with parsley and onion tops for garnish. Serve over cooked rice, usually one cup of rice per serving.

*6 servings*

**Do not overcook seafood. Leftovers reheated the next day after refrigeration usually have more flavor than freshly cooked gumbo. Serve with French bread or hard rolls and salad or potato salad as side dishes.**

*Over the years the mass media has often portrayed the Cajun people as backwoods, simpleminded folks. Cajuns will often play along with the misperception...with an usual twist for the person who mistakes the Cajun for slow-witted. Beaver Club members cite this incident as proof of the Cajun's cunning mind and shrewd thinking:*

*"A counterfeiter was lost in the swampy Louisiana bayou country one day when he came upon a Cajun who owned a gas station along the rural Bayou Self. 'I am almost out of gas,' the counterfeiter told the Cajun. 'Can you make change for the 12 dollar bill so I can buy some gas from you?' The Cajun replied, 'Mais, sure. Now do you want dat in three 4s, four 3s or two 6 dollar bills?"*

# CHICKEN SAUSAGE FILÉ GUMBO

1 3 pound chicken, boiled in 2½ quarts of water and deboned (Save stock for gumbo)
1 pound smoke sausage, cut in ½ inch slices
2 tablespoons water
2 tablespoons oil
2 celery ribs, chopped
2 cloves garlic, minced
2 medium onions, chopped
¼ cup fresh parsley, chopped
2 medium onions, chopped
¼ cup green onions, minced
1 teaspoon Worcestershire sauce
3 tablespoons browning sauce
1 cup medium brown roux
2 teaspoons corn starch
salt and red pepper to taste
add filé to each individual serving of gumbo. Do not cook in gumbo as it will make soup stringy.

Boil stock and vegetables except green onions, parsley, and garlic for 5 minutes. Reduce to medium heat and cook for 15 minutes. In skillet, fry sausage with water and oil, allowing water to evaporate before frying begins. When light brown put into stock pot. Put chopped up chicken, garlic, seasonings except pepper. Simmer for 1 hour. Add pepper, parsley, green onions, Worcestershire sauce, browning sauce and resalt as needed to adjust taste. Dissolve corn starch in 2 tablespoons of water; stir into gumbo. Simmer 5 minutes then turn off fire and keep covered. Skim off excess oil. Serve over fluffy long grain rice as a soup.

*6 servings*

## CHICKEN AND SAUSAGE GUMBO

2 chickens, deboned
1 pound half-inch slices of smoked sausage
2 cups chopped green onions
3 cups chopped white onions
1½ cup chopped bell pepper
3 cups chopped okra
½ cup flour
½ cup cooking oil
1 tablespoon filé gumbo
5 cups water

Boil and debone chicken. Prepare roux by mixing oil and flour together, cooking until it reaches the color of a copper penny. Be careful not to burn. Add seasonings and cook until the onions clarify (become translucent). Add five cups of water. Add the deboned chicken and sausage to the pot. Salt and pepper to taste. Bring to a boil and simmer for one hour.

## OKRA GUMBO

6 quarts fresh okra
polyunsaturated cooking oil, enough to cover bottom of pot
2 onions
1 can tomatoes with chiles
1 or 2 dashes garlic powder
chicken, seafood, tasso sausage, etc.
salt, red pepper and black pepper to taste
rice

Wash okra, slice in thin pieces. Cover the bottom of a Dutch oven with oil. Cook on medium until okra no longer "slimes". You must stir often. Do expect sticking. Okra will no longer be green but brownish. After okra is cooked, add tomatoes and onion, cook until onion is wilted. Do not cover. Add about 3 to 4 inches of water to pot. Season with salt, black pepper and red pepper, if desired. Add one or two dashes of garlic powder. Simmer until boiling. At this time add chicken pieces, seafood, etc. Gumbo should more than cover chicken (meat). Cook until meat is cooked. Chicken will take about 1½ hours. Just before chicken is cooked, add additional chopped onions. Serve over rice when onion is wilted.

**If gumbo is too thick, just add water. If too green in color, add browning sauce.**

## COURIR DE MARDI GRAS

Cajun country's traditional courir de Mardi Gras is perhaps the world's most distinctive Shrove Tuesday observance. Using begging rituals dating back to the Middle Ages, participants in the courir de Mardi Gras travel on horseback or, less commonly, in tractor-drawn trailers, along designated routes, stopping at each residence along the way. At the entrance of each residence's driveway, "captains"—titular leaders of the roving revelers—hold aloft a flag to request the householder's permission to approach the house. There, before the house, the assembled revelers appeal for ingredients to a communal gumbo to be prepared upon the revelers' return to their home base (usually in a nearby town). Householders routinely agree to make a donation, but only after the revelers have danced for their dinner. Once the ritual dance is complete, the householders usually release a live chicken (The hosts less commonly donate Cajun sausage or rice.); the costumed riders immediately give chase and inevitably catch the chicken, to the delight of all. The prize is presented to the captain, the revelers mount their horses, and the procession makes its way to the next house along the route.

# TEAL DUCK AND OYSTER GUMBO

6 teal, dressed
4 dozen raw oysters
2 cups of flour
2 cups of vegetable oil
salt, red pepper, and black
  pepper to taste
2 onions, chopped fine

2 bell peppers, chopped
1 stalk of celery, chopped
  fine
1 pack onion tops, cut fine
1 stalk parsley flakes, cut
  fine
1 pound butter

Cut up teal ducks into pieces, season to taste, and brown in a large black skillet. Set aside and drain off excess grease. Mix flour and oil slowly in a large Dutch oven on top of stove over a low fire, stirring constantly with a wooden spoon, being careful not to let mixture stick or smoke. Stir roux mix until it becomes almost black (approximately 20 to 30 minutes). Add chopped onions, celery, and bell peppers into roux and cook until onions get clear. Next, add about 6 cups of cold water to separate the vegetables from the roux. Add cut up duck pieces and cook over a slow fire for approximately 2½ to 3 hours (until meat becomes tender). Keep adding water from time to time. Do not let gumbo get too thick. Approximately 20 minutes before serving gumbo, add the onion tops and parsley as well as the raw oysters. Remember to also add approximately ½ of the oyster juice to the gumbo.

*Serve with white rice, French bread, and potato salad.*

*Approximately 8 servings*

# GUMBO AT THE GOVERNOR'S BALL, 1803

Gumbos were first described by travelers along the Mississippi River around 1803. Then as now, there were evidently as many varieties of gumbo as there were gumbo cooks. Some cooks used okra—known locally by its African appellation, gumbo—in the soup, thereby forever affixing the vegetable's name to Louisiana's "national" dish. Prefect Pierre Clément de Laussat, sent in 1803 by Napoleon Bonaparte to prepare Louisiana for the arrival of a French army of occupation, recorded in his memoirs that during the course of one social gathering he attended "twenty-four gumbos were served, six or eight of which were sea turtle."

## SPOONBILL AND DEER SAUSAGE GUMBO

6 spoonbills
1 pound deer sausage
6 onions
1 stalk celery
1 bell pepper
1 clove garlic

safflower oil
whole wheat flour
Tamari sauce
red pepper and salt to taste
brown rice

Cut up duck into quarters (you may want to cut the breast in half). Stuff duck with garlic. Season with red pepper and Tamari generously. Put enough oil to cover bottom of gumbo pot and place on high heat and brown ducks. After ducks are brown, put them in another bowl. Brown sausage without cutting it up. Deer sausage which is deer meat mixed with pork sausage is much tastier than smoked sausage in gumbo. You must be careful not to cut it up, or it will come apart in the cooking process. When sausage is brown, take out and place in bowl with the ducks. Place enough whole wheat flour until consistency is still liquid, but almost solid. Stir constantly until roux has a nutty smell and is as dark as possible, without being burned. Immediately add chopped onions, bell pepper, celery, and the remainder of the garlic, stirring constantly. Then add the ducks and sausage and 1 cup of water at a time. When water begins to come to a boil, add another cup until the thickness of the gumbo is right. Continue adding water and seasoning and cook for at least 2 to 3 hours on medium heat. Add salt to taste. When you start cooking your brown rice, add a bunch of chopped green onions.

*Serve and enjoy with a good glass of red wine.*

# SHRIMP AND CORN SOUP

1 16 ounce can whole
  kernel corn
5 tablespoons oil
4 tablespoons flour
2 pounds fresh shrimp,
  peeled and deveined (save
  peelings for stock)
2 tablespoons parsley,
  minced
6 shallots, chopped
1 large bell pepper, chopped

1 large onion, chopped
2 ribs celery and leaves,
  chopped
1 16 ounce can whole
  tomatoes, drained and
  coarsely chopped
3 cups chicken broth stock
  (add more for thinner
  soup)
1 teaspoon ground basil
salt and pepper to taste

Make a golden brown roux in pot with flour and oil. Stir frequently on low fire. In another pot add chicken stock and shrimp peelings and medium boil for 3 minutes. Strain into roux pot. Add tomatoes, onion, bell pepper, and celery. Low simmer for 20 minutes. Stir frequently to prevent tomato burning. Add all ingredients except shrimp, parsley, and shallots. Simmer for 40 minutes. Add shrimp and shallots. Simmer 10 minutes. Adjust seasonings and thickness. Turn fire off. Add parsley.

*6 servings*

# MUSHROOM SOUP LA CRÈME

1 pound fresh mushrooms,
  sliced
8 tablespoons flour
1½ stick butter
2 bay leaves
1 quart milk
1½ quarts chicken stock

1 large onion, chopped
1 bunch green onions,
  finely chopped
½ teaspoon pepper sauce
4 chicken bouillon cubes
1 cup celery, finely chopped

Boil onion, bay leaves, celery and tops of green onions in the stock for ¾ hour. Substitute with canned chicken stock if desired. Add chicken bouillon cubes to strengthen stock. Strain in a heavy pot. Melt butter over low heat and add flour. Cook 5 minutes, stirring constantly. Slowly add milk. When mix is creamy, slowly add stock. Simmer 10 minutes. Add mushrooms, salt and pepper, and pepper sauce. Simmer 5 minutes. Serve warm. Garnish each bowl with chopped green onions.

## CREOLE VEGETABLE SOUP

6-8 pounds soup meat or brisket (*get larger for a bonus dish the next day)
2 16 ounce cans whole tomatoes, chopped
7 quarts water
4 large onions, coarsely chopped
2 potatoes, quartered
6 medium carrots, coarsely chopped
6 ribs celery and leaves, chopped

½ pound dry green lima beans
6 ears corn on the cob, cut into fourths
¾ cup shallots
2 tablespoons pepper sauce
¾ teaspoon thyme
4 bay leaves
1 tablespoon garlic powder
salt, black and red pepper to taste

Cut meat into 3 inch chunks and place in 10 quart pot with all ingredients. Bring to boil then reduce to simmer. Cook for approximately 4 hours until meat is tender. Stir occasionally to remove scum from top. Add more water if desired.

*Now the bonus dish to enjoy the next day is...serve the extra soup meat with Creole mustard or horseradish with boiled buttered Irish potatoes garnished with fresh parsley.*

*12 servings*

## VICHYSSOISE

6 leeks, thinly sliced
1½ cup Half and Half cream
1 cup milk
6 medium onions, thinly sliced
2½ pounds potatoes, peeled and thinly sliced

2 sticks butter
2 tablespoons chopped chives or shallots
2 tablespoons green shallot tops, chopped
salt and pepper to taste

Melt butter in deep pan and then on low fire. Sauté green onions and leeks until they are soft. Add potatoes and water to cover them. Bring to a boil, then reduce heat and simmer for 1 hour. Remove from fire, press through a sieve and refrigerate at least an hour. Just before serving, add cold cream and milk. Add salt and pepper; mix. Sprinkle with chives and serve cold.

*6 servings*

# BAYOU TURTLE SOUP

3 pounds turtle meat
1 teaspoon black pepper
8 tablespoons flour
1 large onion, chopped
1 cup shallots, chopped
2 large tomatoes, chopped coarse
½ cup celery with tops, chopped
3 large bell peppers, chopped
6 cloves garlic, chopped
2 teaspoons cloves
2 teaspoons thyme
2 bay leaves
¼ teaspoon All Spice
¼ teaspoon nutmeg, grated
1½ cup water
4 cups beef stock (or 5 cans beef consommé)
2 lemons, thin sliced
6 tablespoons sherry wine
2 teaspoons Worcestershire sauce
¼ cup parsley, chopped
¼ cup green onion tops, chopped
3 hard boiled eggs, sliced

Melt butter in heavy pot on low heat; add flour, stirring frequently to prevent burning. When roux is medium brown, add onions, tomatoes, celery, bell pepper and garlic. Cook on low heat 30 minutes until vegetables brown. Chop meat in small pieces then add along with salt, black pepper, red pepper, bay leaves, thyme, cloves, All Spice, grated nutmeg, beef stock and water. Bring to boil and then lower to simmer. Cook 2½ hours. 30 minutes before soup is done, add Worcestershire, lemon and sherry. Turn off fire and add parsley and green onion tops. Add more water if needed. Prior to serving, add sliced eggs. Serve with toasted garlic French bread.

*4 servings*

*Most Cajuns are raised good Catholics, so they take marriage seriously. But, hunting and fishing are also important to good Cajuns in order to catch those wonderful foods that they grew up eating. You'll note in this classified ad that a Cajun recently put in a local paper that Cajun food must have a high priority:*

*"Eligible Bachelor wants: Woman who can cook, sew, take care of house and who has a boat and outboard motor. Please send photo of boat and motor!"*

## CAJUN BOUILLABAISSE SOUP

1 pound crabmeat
1 pound crawfish tails
4 pounds filleted fish (try to get at least 3 species such as red fish, snapper, catfish, trout, drum cut into 3 inch pieces, save head and bones for fish stock)
1 pound shrimp, peeled and deveined
2 dozen raw oysters (save oyster water)
6 small soft shell crabs (browned in 2 tablespoons of butter and 2 tablespoons of oil then cut cross wise (optional)
1 quart fish stock
½ stick butter (non salt)
8 tablespoons olive oil (save 2 tablespoons for tomatoes)
2 large white onions
2 medium carrots

1 can tomato sauce
3 bay leaves
1 bunch green onions, finely chopped
4 ribs celery, finely chopped
4 cloves garlic, minced
2 tablespoons flour
2 tablespoons minced parsley
4 medium whole tomatoes, peeled and rough chopped
3 cups chicken broth
1 teaspoon salt
1 teaspoon red pepper
½ teaspoon black pepper
1 teaspoon powdered thyme
¼ teaspoon ground All-Spice
¼ teaspoon chili powder
¾ cup dry white wine
⅛ teaspoon saffron
¼ teaspoon ground cloves
peelings from ½ lemon
2 tablespoons lemon juice

Make fish stock with shrimp peelings and fish heads and bones from fillet fish. Remove eyes, scales, entrails, etc. Before boiling in 2 quarts of water. Add bay leaves, green onion tops, and carrots. Boil for 20 minutes. While this is cooking put 2 teaspoons of oil in a skillet and sauté fresh and canned tomato sauce at simmer heat. Stir frequently to keep from sticking. Add two tablespoons of water each time it gets too thick to stir. Cook 30 minutes, then include in main pot and continue to cook until completion of dish. Strain stock through cheese cloth or strainer. Throw residue away. In pot melt butter and add the olive oil. Add green onions bottoms, celery, garlic, and parsley and sauté on low fire for 8 minutes. Stir in flour and cook 5 minutes. Add, salt, red pepper and strained fish stock, plus the chicken broth, bring this to a rolling boil and then lower the heat and simmer for 25 minutes. While this is cooking rub the fillets with salt and black pepper and lemon juice. Bake in a 350°F oven for 15 minutes.

After 25 minutes, add the shrimp, oysters and their water, crawfish, crabmeat, and fried soft shell crabs and slivered peelings of lemon to the pot. Simmer for 5 minutes. Add the baked fillets and cook for 5 more minutes. Re-season as needed. Serve soup over fluffy rice or on top of toasted garlic French bread.

*12 servings*

## DAMN GOOD CRAB BISQUE

1 stick butter
1 large onion
1 bell pepper
6 large fat boiled crabs
3 stalks celery with leaves, finely chopped
1 clove garlic, minced
6 green onions, chopped
2 bay leaves

2 quarts chicken stock (or 6, 10½ ounces of chicken broth)
1 pint Half and Half cream
¼ teaspoon powdered thyme
½ pound lump crabmeat
1 6 ounce can claw meat
salt, red pepper to taste

Clean crabs and cut segments in halves. Melt butter and on low heat sauté onion, garlic, bell pepper, celery, and green onions until opaque, approximately 10 minutes. Add crab segments and sauté for 5 minutes. Sprinkle in enough flour to make roux, about 5 minutes. Add chicken stock or broth, bay leaves, and salt and pepper. Strain sauce (optional). Add the crabmeat and serve with toasted slices of garlic French bread.

*8 servings*

## CORN AND CRAB BISQUE

1 pound crabmeat
2 packs frozen onions
1 stick butter
2 cans Cream of Potato soup
1 fresh whole tomato

2 cans cream style corn
1 pack frozen whole kernel corn
2 tablespoons flour diluted in 2 cups water
Worcestershire sauce

Sauté onion and butter 5 to 10 minutes. Add potato soup, cream style corn, and whole kernel corn. Add a "few dashes" of Worcestershire sauce. Cook 10 to 15 minutes. Add flour diluted in water, chopped tomato and a "few more dashes" of Worcestershire sauce. Let cook about 1 hour on low fire. Stir often, add crabmeat about 30 minutes before serving.

# SPLIT PEA SOUP

1 large ham bone (with some ham still on bone)
½-1 pound nice "chunks" ham
1 pound pack dried green split peas
2½ quarts (10 cups) cold water (more, if needed to cover bone)
1 large white onion, chopped
3-4 celery stalks, chopped
3-4 carrots, thinly sliced
1 clove garlic, minced
a few slices of thinly sliced lemon may be added while soup is simmering
4-6 tablespoons parsley, minced
2 cups chicken broth

Rinse peas under cold water and pick over. In large soup pot, place peas, water and ham bone; start cooking on medium to high heat. In skillet, melt a tablespoon or two of butter or oleo, and sauté onions until slightly brown; add celery, carrots and minced garlic — cook another five minutes or so. By this time, soup water should be simmering, so add sautéed vegetable mixture and 2 cups of chicken broth. Reduce heat to medium and simmer gently for about 2 or 2½ hours. Skim foam which forms on top during this cooking time. After about 2 hours, meat generally begins separating from bone — remove it, cut meat into bite-sized pieces and discard bone. Skim off any fat on surface of soup and adjust seasoning. Salt never seems necessary; however, red and/or black pepper, even a teaspoon of Worcestershire sauce, can be added to taste. Return ham pieces to soup again together with chopped parsley and heat for another five minutes or so.

*Serve piping hot with croutons.*

**Sometimes after cooking and when it is allowed to "sit" a while, the soup "separates" with water at the top...you can "bind" the soup — melt 1 tablespoon or so of butter (or oleo) in saucepan, with 1 tablespoon flour, slowly add cup or two of soup mixture. Cook and stir to boiling and then stir into soup; a scant spoonful or two of potato flakes dissolved in a bit of the soup and then added to the pot will do the same thing!**

# CREOLE SPINACH SALAD

1 pound fresh spinach,
washed and dried
6 bacon strips, fried crisp
4 tablespoons olive oil
2 tablespoons salad oil
4 drops pepper sauce
4 green onions, minced
½ pound fresh mushrooms,
sliced

1 tablespoon Creole
mustard
1 boiled egg, chopped
¼ cup Parmesan cheese,
grated
1 chapon (a slice of dry
French bread rubbed with
fresh garlic cloves)
salt and black pepper to
taste

Be sure spinach is dry. Set aside in 2 quart salad bowl with chapon. Fry bacon strips crisp, remove and chop very finely. Discard bacon drippings from skillet and add olive and salad oil, pepper sauce and green onions. Sauté for 3 minutes. While hot, add mixture to spinach and thoroughly mix. Discard chapon. Salt and pepper to taste. Top with bacon, egg, and Parmesan cheese.

*Served with toasted garlic French bread, this salad could easily be the main course. The magic of the seasoning combination converts the nutritious bland spinach into a tasty culinary delight. The salad is a suitable complement to salads called for in Italian entrées.*

# LÉ CAJUN COLE SLAW

1 large cabbage, washed and finely shredded
½ cup olive oil
2 beef bouillon cubes
1 medium onion, finely chopped
1 bunch green onions
3 tablespoons parsley, minced

1 tablespoon dried basil
¼ teaspoon powdered thyme
4 cloves garlic, minced
3 tablespoons wine vinegar
4 drops hot pepper sauce
salt and black pepper to taste

Place dry shredded cabbage in 6 quart salad bowl and pour over it ½ of olive oil. Mix until all of cabbage is coated with oil. Dissolve the 2 bouillon cubes in 2 tablespoons of simmering water. Allow to cool. Then pour over the cabbage. Add all ingredients except salt and pepper. Toss until mixed. Add salt and pepper to taste. Keep covered in refrigerator.

*8 servings*

**The wonderful blend of seasonings in this cole slaw is typical of the Cajun's cooking instinct. His good luck to pick a superb combination of condiments to tantalize the taste buds is uncanny. Such is the Lé Cajun Cole Slaw recipe. This dish can easily replace any meal which calls for a green salad.**

*Many Cajun meals are based on foods which are hunted in the swamps and bayous of South Louisiana just as in the days when the Acadian people first came to Louisiana from Nova Scotia. Cajuns are good hunters and take pride in that, but a Beaver Club member notes that there is one thing that Cajuns just can't hunt:*

*"Try as they may, Cajuns just can't hunt elephants in Cajun Country. It seems like the decoys are just too heavy for their pirogues!!"*

# WILTED CABBAGE (COLESLAW)

| | |
|---|---|
| 1 medium head cabbage, shredded or 2 small heads | 1 large white onion, chopped finely |
| | ¾ cup sugar |

Toss well in very large bowl (with lid to which hot dressing may be added).

**Topping:**

| | |
|---|---|
| 1 teaspoon celery seed | 1½ teaspoon salt |
| 1 teaspoon sugar | 1 cup white vinegar |
| 1 teaspoon dry mustard | 1 cup oil |

In small saucepan, bring to a full boil; then add 1 cup oil. Bring to second boil; continue boiling for a minute or so. Pour hot dressing over slaw mixture. Toss well several times. Cover tightly and refrigerate, preferably overnight. Should be tossed again a time or two during "holding" time in refrigerator. Drain off some of excess dressing before serving, but reserve to re-add to any leftover. Keeps in refrigerator almost indefinitely! (Optional: finely chopped red and green bell peppers add to taste and provide a bit of color! Garnish with slices of boiled eggs, or with halves of deviled eggs.)

*6-8 servings*

*This is a cabbage recipe for people who think they don't like cabbage. It's at least a quantum leap beyond any coleslaw you've ever tasted.*

# FRESH SPINACH SALAD AND DRESSING

**Fresh Spinach Salad:**

1 pound fresh spinach
1 small red onion, sliced
   thin

3 hard-cooked eggs, finely
   chopped
6 slices bacon, cooked and
   crumbled

Remove stems from spinach, wash leaves in lukewarm water and pat dry. Tear into bite size pieces; combine spinach, onion, eggs and bacon in large bowl. Serve with dressing.

*6 to 8 servings*

**Dressing:**

1 small onion, chopped
1 cup vegetable oil
⅓ cup tarragon vinegar
⅓ cup sugar

1 tablespoon prepared
   mustard
1 teaspoon celery seeds
½ teaspoon salt
½ teaspoon lemon pepper

Combine all ingredients in container of electric blender. Process well and chill. Stir before serving.

*2 cups*

# CURRIED FRUIT

1 can chunky fruit
1 large can pineapple
   chunks
1 large can sliced peaches
1 small can apricots
1 small can sliced pears

Maraschino cherries and
   pitted sweet cherries, as
   desired
2 bananas, sliced
½ cup brown sugar
1 tablespoon corn starch
1 teaspoon curry
¼ cup oleo, melted

Drain canned fruit (and cherries) well (for at least 1-2 hours). Mix brown sugar, corn starch, and curry. Sprinkle over fruit. Pour melted oleo over fruit. Bake uncovered 40 minutes at 350°F.

## 24-HOUR VEGETABLE SALAD

2 heads romaine lettuce,
  torn up
1 pint cherry tomatoes
2 packages slivered
  almonds, toasted

1 cup Swiss cheese, grated
½ cup Parmesan cheese,
  grated
4-5 slices cooked bacon,
  crumbled

Layer in large bowl, cover with plastic wrap, and refrigerate 24 hours.

**Dressing:**
3 large cloves garlic,
  mashed
½ cup oil

1 teaspoon salt
1 lemon, juice only

Mix all together and let stand covered at least 3 hours. Add to salad and toss just before serving.

## CATALINA SALAD

1 head iceberg lettuce,
  chopped
1 medium onion, chopped
  fine
3 medium tomatoes,
  chopped
1 8 ounce bottle Catalina or
  Italian dressing
10 ounces cheddar cheese,
  grated
1 medium bag corn chips
1 10½ ounce can black
  olives, pitted

1 teaspoon salt
½ teaspoon fresh, coarsely
  ground black pepper
⅛ teaspoon cumin
1 teaspoon dry parsley
lemon garlic butter
8 tablespoons butter
1 teaspoon lemon juice
1 teaspoon dry parsley
⅛ teaspoon garlic powder
1 clove garlic, minced

Mix all ingredients except lettuce and chips. Chill several hours before use. Add chips and lettuce and serve with melba toast rounds and lemon garlic butter.

*6 servings*

**This is an excellent dish to serve with a Mexican theme dinner party.**

## CREAMY FROZEN FRUIT SALAD

2 cups sour cream
2 tablespoons lemon juice
¾ cup sugar
pinch salt
1 9 ounce can crushed
   pineapple

¼ cup sliced Maraschino
   cherries
¼ cup pecans
1 banana, sliced

Mix all together and freeze, slice and serve.


## CLETUS' SPANISH MACKEREL SALAD

2 small (or 1 large) mackerels 4-6 eggs
   cut in large chunks

Boil for about 5 minutes in salted water, or until flaky. Drain in colander and cover with ice to cool immediately. When cooled, remove skin and flake off meat, removing undesirable parts. In the meantime, boil 4-6 eggs and mix the following:

½ cup onion top, chopped
½ cup parsley, chopped
½ cup celery, chopped
½ cup olives, chopped
½ cup boiled eggs, chopped

Mash egg yolks and add
   juice of 1 lemon
2 tablespoons mayonnaise
1 teaspoon Dijon mustard
salt, pepper, garlic powder
   to taste

Mix thoroughly. Gently fold in flaked fish. Add mayonnaise if necessary. Chill before serving. Serve as a sandwich or on lettuce leaves.

*Very often we catch mackerel when fishing for speckled trout. This is an excellent use for them.*

## LA CRÈME FRENCH DRESSING

¼ teaspoon salt
¼ teaspoon black pepper
1 teaspoon dijon mustard
1 tablespoon shallots,
   chopped fine

1 teaspoon fresh parsley,
   minced
3 tablespoons vinegar
⅓ cup heavy cream
1 teaspoon lemon juice

Combine all ingredients except lemon juice and cream. Mix well. Slowly add cream and lemon juice, mixing well. Refrigerate. Shake well before using.

*1 cup*

***This creamy dressing is excellent on cabbage slaw or on steamed broccoli.***

## FIVE N' ONE VINAIGRETTE DRESSING

¼ teaspoon salt
¼ teaspoon black pepper
1 teaspoon dijon mustard
1 tablespoon shallots,
   minced

1 teaspoon parsley,
   chopped
3 tablespoons vinegar
8 teaspoons olive oil
1 teaspoon lemon juice

Add all ingredients in a bowl except lemon juice and olive oil. Mix well. Whisk as olive oil is poured in a thin stream. Now add lemon juice and stir. Refrigerate. Shake well before serving. If garlic, basil, herb mix or mint flavors are desired, add during first step of preparation.

*1 cup*

## FRONEY'S ROQUEFORT CHEESE DRESSING

½ teaspoon garlic salt
½ teaspoon celery salt
½ teaspoon black pepper
½ teaspoon paprika

2 tablespoons vinegar
1 pint sour cream
½ cup mayonnaise
1 teaspoon salt

Mix above ingredients well. Crumble and blend in carefully a small wedge of Roquefort cheese and wedge of Blue cheese.

## FRENCH SALAD DRESSING

3 large shallots or green onions, chopped very finely
1 stalk celery (this might be a little too much)
liberal amount parsley
1 teaspoon salt
½ teaspoon freshly ground black pepper

½ teaspoon dried sweet basil
pinch rosemary
pinch marjoram
1⅓ cups olive oil or salad oil
⅔ cups tarragon flavored red wine vinegar

Chop shallots, celery and parsley together until as fine as coffee grounds. Combine this with the remaining ingredients and let dressing stand for several hours.

*Be sure that red wine vinegar is tarragon flavored.*

*With the close proximity of their home states, Texans and Cajuns often indulge in a little friendly competition and one-upmanship. Actually they are great friends who share a fondness for the great outdoors, spicy foods, and a little down-home humor:*

*"Ol' Tex was bragging to Boudreaux about his wealth. You see, Ol' Tex had a large, oil-laden cattle ranch in El Paso. Boudreaux was a 40-acre crawfish and rice farmer. 'Yep, Boo-droh,' said Ol' Tex, 'when I get in my truck to ride out over my ranch, it takes me all the day just to ride across it.' To which Boudreaux good-naturedly responded, 'I can sympathize with dat, my friend. I got a truck that don't run so good either!' "*

# CAJUN COUNTRY BOY

The early life experiences of ninety-eight-year-old Claude Hébert, a retired high school agriculture teacher presently residing in Scott, mirror the life and times of other Cajun men of his generation. Claude, his younger brother, and his sister were reared by their parents on a forty-acre farm near Youngsville, Lafayette Parish, Louisiana. As a young man, Claude worked very hard, growing cotton, corn, and farm animals. He labored from dawn to dusk, doing both field chores and the family milking, a job he did himself because he knew that his timid cows would produce less milk for strange hands. To maximize milk production, Hébert always made a calf suckle its mother first to bring down the cow's milk; Claude then tied the calf alongside its mother who licked her baby contentedly while Hébert milked her. Claude Hébert usually maintained ten to twelve cattle on the farm for milk and meat production and for sale at market.

Claude's dad participated in the local communal butchery, which furnished and processed meat for local families in the years before refrigeration. The *boucherie de la campagne* (country butchery) assured a group of thirty-two farmers—divided into four equal work squads—that their families would have fresh meat twice a week. Participating families furnished, on a rotating basis, an animal large enough to provide each household with five to ten pounds of meat; the animal's owner received the internal organs. In winter, hogs were slaughtered for fresh meat and for the production of salt meat, sausage, hog head cheese, cracklin, boudin, and other products.

**61**

Claude recalls that Jean Jacques Hébert, his grandfather, had a club foot, the result of a childhood accident. A loaded wagon crushed his foot, but no doctor was available to set the bones.

Jean Jacques Hébert operated a grist mill which ground corn and beans during the Civil War, when area residents had no access to flour and coffee. Beans were parched for coffee-making. (Jean Jacques normally charged his customers one-fourth of the grain and beans they ground for use of the mill, but this fee did not apply to widows and orphans of slain soldiers.) Syrup replaced sugar as a sweetener after slaves escaped from the plantations, and there was insufficient manpower to run local sugar mills. Sweet potatoes became a major source of starch during the war. Sweet potato production later became a major Louisiana industry.

Claude Hébert, who views modern changes with considerable skepticism, reveres these fond memories. "We must not forget our Cajun roots," he maintains.

# MEN COOK
# VEGETABLES

# VEGETABLES

# RANCH BEANS À LA JOHN DAIGRE

2 pounds ground chuck
1 large onion, chopped
2 stalks celery, finely
  chopped
1 20 ounce bottle chili
  powder
1 teaspoon salt
¼ teaspoon pepper
1 16 ounce can pork and
  beans

½ cup catsup
½ cup honey
4 teaspoons brown or
  granulated sugar
¼ teaspoon garlic powder
4 tablespoons parsley
¼ cup white wine
½ pound processed cheese
  spread

Brown ground chuck. Add onions and celery and cook over low heat in covered pot until tender, approximately 20 minutes. Add chili powder, salt and pepper and cook over low heat for approximately 20 minutes. Stir as needed to prevent sticking. Add remaining ingredients and cook over low heat for approximately 1 hour, stirring to prevent sticking.

*10 servings*

# SWEET BASIL LIMA BEANS

2 bags frozen lima beans
1 block butter or margarine
½ teaspoon dried sweet
  basil

½ teaspoon seasoning salt
2½ cups water

Place beans, butter, sweet basil and seasoning in large Dutch oven. Cover beans with 2½ cups water. Cook covered for 45 minutes on medium heat.

*8 to 10 servings*

**Good to take for large group suppers - covered dish type.**

# RED BEANS AND SAUSAGE

| | |
|---|---|
| 1 pound red beans | 1 bell pepper |
| 1 pound smoked sausage | Creole seasoning to taste |
| 1 large onion | garlic salt to taste |

For best results, soak beans overnight. Next morning rinse and sort beans. The bad ones will be on top. Cover beans with at least one or two inches of water, then start to cook over low heat with cover on. Next, slice sausage and put it in skillet to brown. Drain all juice before adding sausage to beans. In same skillet, sauté onions and bell pepper until clear; add to beans and sausage. Season with Creole seasoning and garlic salt to taste. Raise heat to medium, cover pot and cook. Stir beans frequently, continue to add water, if needed. After beans are soft, mash about 2 tablespoons of beans to make a thick creamy liquid. Add to beans. Serve with rice or cornbread.

*6 servings*

# SWEET POTATO SOUFFLÉ

**Potatoes:**

| | |
|---|---|
| 4 cup mashed sweet potatoes | ⅓ cup melted butter/margarine |
| ½ cup sugar | ½ cup milk |
| ½ teaspoon salt | 1 teaspoon vanilla |
| | 2 eggs |

Boil sweet potatoes. Peel and mash. Mix all ingredients and put into 9x13 inch casserole.

**Topping:**

| | |
|---|---|
| ⅓ cup margarine | ⅓ cup flour |
| 1 cup light brown sugar | 1 cup chopped pecans |

Melt margarine. Mix together ingredients for topping. Pour melted margarine into mixture and stir until mixed well. Spoon onto casserole. Bake on upper rack of oven at 350°F uncovered for 1 hour or until top is brown. The crispier the topping, the better.

# D. LANDRY'S SWEET POTATO CASSEROLE

**Potatoes:**

3 cup mashed sweet
  potatoes-approximately 6-
  7 medium (can use canned
  or microwaved fresh ones)

½ cup butter
⅓ cup milk
1 teaspoon vanilla
2 eggs

Mix all ingredients together well and place in a 9 x 13 inch baking dish.

**Topping:**

⅓ cup melted butter
½ cup flour

1 cup light brown sugar
1 cup chopped pecans

Mix all ingredients together and place on top of the sweet potatoes. Bake at 350°F for 30 minutes.

# DAVID'S POTATO CASSEROLE

1 large bag hash brown
  potatoes
½ stick butter
3¼ ounce real bacon bits
1 pint sour cream

1 cup chopped green onions
1 cup chopped white onions
1 pound processed cheese
  spread
Seasonings to taste

In a large pyrex or casserole dish, combine all ingredients except processed cheese spread. Melt processed cheese spread and mix. Bake at 350°F for 50 minutes.

*8-10 servings*

# SHELLING PEAS AND BEANS

In late June and early July, when the cash crops were laid by and when it was too hot to spend much time indoors, Cajun farm families often congregated under shade trees to process produce from their spring gardens. In their own inimitable style, Cajuns overcame the drudgery associated with such dull work by emphasizing the social aspect of the gathering. An almost continuous exchange of jokes, gossip, and local news helped divert workers' attention from their fatigue and the monotony of their tasks.

## BAKED POTATO DISH

1 bag frozen hash browns,
  thawed
1 pint sour cream
2 cups sharp cheese,
  shredded

1 can cream celery soup
½ cup butter or margarine,
  melted
2 cup corn flakes, crushed

Combine all ingredients and pour into 13 x 9 inch microwave dish. Crush 2 cups corn flakes and mix with ½ cup butter or margarine. Spread this mixture on top of hash brown mixture. Bake for 1 hour at 350°F.

*6+ servings*

*Very good as a leftover too.*

## OLD FASHIONED SNAP BEANS AND NEW POTATOES

1 pound fresh snap beans
5 small new potatoes
1 large onion

3 slices bacon
2 cloves garlic
Creole seasoning

Remove tips from snap beans, snap in half and soak in water for 1 to 2 hours. Peel potatoes and cut each into 2 or 3 parts. Cut bacon into small pieces and place over bottom of a 3 quart saucepan. Finely chop onion and garlic and place over bacon. Cook bacon, onion and garlic over medium heat until onions are very tender. Add snap beans and potatoes to saucepan and mix well. Fill with water until mixture is totally covered. Place sauce pan on stove top and bring water to boil on high heat. Reduce heat to low, cover and simmer for 45 minutes. Season to taste with Creole seasoning. Continue to simmer covered for an additional 45 minutes. Check occasionally to ensure adequate liquid. Drain and serve in heated bowl.

*4-6 servings*

*This same recipe works just as well with 1 pound package of freshly frozen baby lima beans as it does with snap beans and potatoes.*

# BUTCHER'S HOT SHOT POTATOES

1 cup onion, chopped
6 tablespoons butter
2 pounds frozen hash brown
  potatoes
1 10¾ ounce can cream of
  mushroom soup
2 cups sharp cheddar
  cheese, grated

1½ cup sour cream
¼ cup mayonnaise
¼ teaspoon salt
⅛ teaspoon cayenne red
  pepper
2 cups Rice Krispies cereal,
  crushed
¼ stick butter, melted

Sauté onion in 6 tablespoons butter. In a bowl combine rest of ingredients except cereal and ¼ stick butter. Mix well. Spread in 13x8x2 inch baking dish. Evenly distribute cereal and unmelted butter on top. Bake in oven at 350°F for 1 hour and 15 minutes.

*12 servings*

*This excellent flavored potato dish is universal in usage. It is compatible with barbecue, fish and chicken fries, or as a main starch vegetable for breakfast, lunch or dinner.*

**Add a 4 ounce jar of chopped pimentos to the mix to enrich the flavor even more.**

# OUTDOOR POTATOES

4 medium potatoes
1 small onion, thinly sliced
⅛ teaspoon garlic powder

½ stick oleo
Creole seasoning to taste

Wash and cube potatoes (about 1 inch square). Do not peel. Place in several sheets of aluminum foil or on aluminum pie tin. Add all other ingredients. Wrap tightly with foil. Place on hot barbecue grill. Cook approximately 1 hour. Cut open foil and serve.

*4 servings*

## CAJUN HOT POTATOES

6 pounds small new
 potatoes
6 ounces liquid crab boil

3 sticks oleo, melted
4 ounces finely chopped
 garlic

In a large pot (10 quart), place the crab boil and enough water to cover the potatoes. Boil until the potatoes are soft. Drain and put them in a container with a cover. If any potatoes are large, cut in half or quarters. Mix oleo and garlic, pour over potatoes, and cover tightly until ready to serve. Stir occasionally.

*15 servings*

**These can be prepared and kept in a small cooler for hours before serving.**

## RICE CASSEROLE

1 can sliced mushrooms
1 can sliced water
 chestnuts

1 can French onion soup
1 stick margarine
1 cup raw rice

Reserve water from chestnuts and mushrooms. Melt margarine in saucepan. Sauté water chestnuts and mushrooms. Combine with raw rice, onion soup, reserved liquid and 1 can water. Bake at 300°F uncovered for 1 hour.

*4-6 servings*

*As further proof that Cajun men do indeed cook, one of the Beaver Club members offers the following recipe for*

### *"OLD-FASHIONED TURKEY STUFFING":*

*3 cups bread crumbs*
*1 teaspoon salt*
*1 teaspoon poultry*
 *seasoning*

*2 cups popping corn*
 *(uncooked)*
*½ cup water*
*2 grated onions*

*Mix all ingredients until moistened. Fill cavity of turkey and bake for about three hours at 350°F or until the popcorn blows the turkey's derriere across the room.*

## SAVORY RICE DRESSING

1 medium onion, chopped fine
2 stalks celery, chopped fine
½ cup chopped green onions
2 tablespoons soy sauce
1 can cream of mushroom soup
1 can raw rice (use empty soup can)
2 pods garlic, minced
1 bell pepper, chopped fine
¼ cup fresh parsley (cut up)
1 stick margarine
1 can cream of chicken soup
1 pound lean ground meat
salt and pepper to taste

Sauté first 3 ingredients in a heavy skillet on low heat - do not brown. Add ground meat; cook and stir until meat loses its red color. Add other ingredients, mixing well. Pour into buttered casserole. Bake covered at 350°F for 1 hour. Stir every 15 minutes.

*8 servings*

*This is especially good for those who dislike gizzards or liver, which are usually used in rice dressing.*

## CAJUN RICE DRESSING

1 pound ground pork
1 medium onion
½ medium bell pepper
2 teaspoons salt
2 teaspoons black and red pepper
¼ cup cooking oil
2 teaspoons garlic powder
3 cups cooked rice
1 cup chives and parsley

Sauté onions and bell peppers on medium heat. When onions are ready, add 1 pound of ground pork; stir. You must cook and brown pork for at least 45 minutes to an hour. Do not taste for seasoning until meat is fully cooked, then add condiments. Now you are ready to mix in 3 cups of cooked rice. Mix meat and rice and add chives and parsley finely diced and a little black pepper to accent the taste. Salt and pepper to your taste.

*5-8 servings*

# SPINACH MOUSSE

2 10 ounce packages
  frozen, chopped spinach,
  thawed and squeezed dry
4 tablespoons butter
2 cloves minced garlic
3 green onions

2 tablespoons flour
½ cup half & half
½ cup whipping cream
1 teaspoon salt
½ teaspoon black pepper
3 eggs

Preheat oven at 350°F. Butter 6 small pyrex dishes. Melt butter, sauté onions and garlic until wilted. Add flour and stir. Add spinach and seasoning. Cook 5 minutes. Cook slightly. Lightly beat eggs and fold into spinach mixture. Pour into buttered pyrex dishes. Place pyrex in larger pan and add water half-way up sides. Put a piece of buttered parchment paper on top of spinach mixture. Bake 20-30 minutes or until set. Remove from water and carefully unmold unto plates.

*6 servings*

# SPINACH DUMPLINGS

4 tablespoons melted butter
2 10 ounce packages frozen
  spinach
¾ cup Ricotta cheese
2 eggs, lightly beaten
6 tablespoons flour
¾ cup Parmesan cheese

½ teaspoon salt
1 tablespoon salt
½ teaspoon pepper
pinch nutmeg
6-8 quarts water
4 tablespoons butter

Melt the butter and cook spinach two to three minutes, until it sticks lightly to pot. Add Ricotta and cook, stirring for 3 to 4 minutes longer. In large bowl, mix spinach, eggs, flour, ¼ cup of cheese, salt, pepper and nutmeg. Refrigerate 30 minutes to 1 hour or until firm. Flour hands and pick up about 1 tablespoon chilled mixture. Shape into small balls. Gently drop balls in simmering water and cook uncovered five to eight minutes or until they puff slightly. Set on towel to drain. Put 2 tablespoons of butter in shallow 8x12 inch baking dish. Arrange balls in one layer about ¼ inch apart, dribble remaining 2 tablespoons butter over them and sprinkle with remaining ½ cup of cheese. Bake on center shelf of oven for 5 minutes at 350°F and serve at once.

## CAJUN MEXICAN CORN

3 1 pound can cream corn
2 1 pound cans whole
  kernel corn
2 pounds crawfish or
  shrimp meat
1½ cup white corn meal
4 eggs, beaten
2 large onions, chopped fine
3 stalks celery, chopped
  fine
1 large red bell pepper,
  chopped fine, for color
3 tablespoons garlic salt
¼ teaspoon cayenne red
  pepper
½ teaspoon basil
½ teaspoon thyme
1 teaspoon baking powder
¾ cup vegetable oil
1 can cream of mushroom
  soup
2 1 ounce cans chopped
  chile peppers, drained
1 pound sharp cheddar
  cheese, grated

In 4 quart iron pot, heat oil on medium heat and sauté onions, celery, garlic and red bell pepper until onion is limp. Remove and set aside. In a large bowl, mix crawfish or shrimp, mushroom soup, eggs, corn, corn meal, seasonings, and baking powder. In another bowl, mix chopped chile peppers, cheese and sautéed vegetables. Pour mixtures into a 13x9x2 inch baking dish in alternating layers. End up with cheese mix on top. Bake in oven, uncovered, for 45 minutes at 350°F.

*20 servings*

*Talk about a pot luck meal in one dish for a large group. This is it! The flavor is superb.*

**Serve with Mexican corn bread, and a good tossed salad. Top with ice cold watermelon or home made ice cream. It ain't no better.**

# CORN MAQUE CHOUX

4 tablespoons bacon fat or butter

8 cups fresh off the cob sweet corn (preferred), or frozen

1 cup fresh or canned whole tomatoes

2 cups onion, chopped fine

1 cup bell pepper, chopped fine

1 cup chicken stock or chicken bouillon

1 cup milk

1½ teaspoon salt

1 teaspoon sugar

1 teaspoon cayenne red pepper

½ teaspoon garlic powder

1 bay leaf

1 teaspoon basil

1 teaspoon black pepper

Melt bacon fat or butter in 6 quart iron pot. Add one cup corn and parch to a medium brown. Do not burn, about 10 minutes. Strain and set aside. Add to the drippings, all vegetables except corn. Cook on high heat for 10 minutes. Stir frequently to keep from sticking or burning. Add corn and all other ingredients except basil, milk, chicken stock, and sugar. Set aside cup of browned corn. Stir well and cook at high heat, covered, for 5 minutes. Uncover, scrape corn crust from bottom of pot and cook for 5 minutes, continue to stir crust from bottom to prevent burning. Remove bay leaf, add browned corn and continue to cook on high heat for about 10 minutes. Continue to scrape and mix crust formed at the bottom of the pot. Now add chicken stock, milk and sugar. Cover, and simmer on low heat for 15 minutes. If corn is a little dry, add more milk, add basil. Adjust seasoning as needed and simmer for 5 more minutes. Stir occasionally.

*10 servings*

*This is one of the choice corn dishes in southwest Louisiana. Handed down from the Indians, the flavor is outstanding.*

**This dish can easily be converted to a seafood chowder by adding a pound of fresh peeled and deveined shrimp, crawfish or 2 pints small oysters, a quart of light cream and adjusting the seasonings to your liking. Add these ingredients during the last ten minutes of cooking.**

## ZUCCHINI, STUFFED

5 medium zucchini, (about 6 inches)
1 pound ground beef
2 tablespoons vegetable oil
2 tablespoons Worcestershire sauce
1 teaspoon salt
½ teaspoon black pepper
⅛ teaspoon cayenne red pepper
¼ teaspoon garlic powder
¼ teaspoon oregano
1 medium onion, chopped
4 sprigs parsley, chopped
4 sprigs onion tops, chopped
½ medium bell pepper, chopped
3 cloves garlic, chopped
1 teaspoon curry powder
1½ teaspoon commercial hot sauce
1½ cup herb seasoned croutons
1 cup cheddar cheese, grated

Boil zucchini in water until tender. Remove, drain, cool and then remove pulp. Set pulp and shells aside. In a 2 quart sauce pan, heat oil and sauté onion, bell peppers and garlic, about 5 minutes on medium heat. Add meat with seasonings and brown, about 15 minutes on medium heat. Add mashed squash pulp with Worcestershire and hot sauces, onion tops and parsley. Cook on simmer for 30 minutes. Stir as needed. Mix croutons and cheese. Stuff zucchini shells. Place in a 9x9x2 inch baking dish with ¼ inch of water to cover bottom and keep squash moist. Bake in oven until cheese is melted, about 5 minutes. Optional: Sprinkle with Parmesan cheese.

*8 servings*

**Try this with fried eggplant, and asparagus. Top with dinner rolls and wine.**

## SQUASH & ZUCCHINI CASSEROLE

3 large squash
3 large zucchini
1 can cream of mushroom
soup
3 ounces grated cheddar
cheese

3 ounces grated Swiss
cheese
1 teaspoon Italian
seasoning
½ teaspoon ground thyme
½ teaspoon garlic powder

Slice squash and zucchini into ¼ inch thick round pieces. Mix together and spread out in bottom of baking dish. Sprinkle seasonings over the top. Pour cream of mushroom soup evenly over vegetables. Then, evenly spread both cheeses on top of the soup. Bake at 350°F for 15 minutes (longer if don't prefer crispy vegetables). Broccoli and cauliflower can be substituted for squash and zucchini.

*6 x 9 inch baking dish*                    *6-8 servings*

## BUTCHER'S FRIED EGGPLANT

1 medium eggplant, peeled
and cut in ½ inch wide
wedges
⅔ cup seasoned bread
crumbs

⅓ cup Parmesan cheese
1½ teaspoon salt
¼ teaspoon black pepper
2 eggs, beaten
2 tablespoons milk

Mix dry ingredients. Mix egg and milk. Roll eggplant into crumbs, then liquid, then crumbs again. Deep fry at about 350°F and then drain on a baking sheet lined with a brown paper bag. Give full attention to the frying process as eggplant cooks and browns very rapidly. Sprinkle more salt on top of fried eggplant pieces as needed.

*4 servings*

*You will find this is one of the better fried vegetable recipes. Close your eyes while you are sampling; you will think you are eating fried fish.*

**Add this dish to your fried seafood menu. Fits like a glove.**

## EGGPLANT BACON ROLLS

10 slices eggplant, ¼ inch
  thick
1 pound lamb shoulder,
  ground
1 medium onion, minced
¼ cup minced parsley
½ teaspoon monosodium
  glutamate

½ teaspoon salt
Few grains pepper
10 slices bacon
2 beef bouillon cubes
1 cup hot water
1 8 ounce can tomato sauce

Sprinkle eggplant slices generously with salt and let stand about
½ hour or until limp. Rinse thoroughly in cold water. Combine
lamb, onion, parsley, monosodium glutamate, salt, and pepper
and mix well. Place spoonful lamb mixture on each eggplant
slice; roll up; wrap slices of bacon around each roll. Secure rolls
with toothpicks. Dissolve bouillon cubes in hot water. Add tomato sauce and blend. Pour liquid around rolls. Bake in moder-
ate oven (350°F) 1¼ hours, turning rolls at the end of 45 minutes to brown both sides.

*5 servings*

## SAUSAGE STUFFED EGGPLANT

3 chicken bouillon cubes
1½ cup hot water
1⅓ cup precooked rice
2 medium eggplants
⅔ cup buttered bread
  crumbs
½ pound pork sausage

1 small onion, minced
¼ cup chili sauce
1 tablespoon prepared
  horseradish
few drops hot sauce
salt and pepper to taste

Dissolve bouillon cubes in hot water. Cool. Use as liquid in preparing pre-cooked rice according to package directions. Parboil
eggplants for 1 minute. Cool slightly. Cut in ½ lengthwise. Scoop
out pulp, leaving firm shell about ½ inch thick. Chop pulp. Brown
sausage in skillet, add chopped eggplant pulp, and cook slowly
10 minutes. Add cooked rice, onion, chili sauce, horseradish,
salt and pepper. With this mixture, fill eggplant shells and top
with buttered bread crumbs. Bake in 350°F oven for ½ hour.

*8 servings*

# CABBAGE CASSEROLE

| | |
|---|---|
| 1 medium head cabbage | 1 can cream of mushroom |
| 1 pound hot smoked | soup |
| sausage, chopped | 1½ cup cooked rice |
| 1 medium onion, chopped | ¼ cup crushed potato chips |
| 3 cloves garlic, chopped | |

Cut cabbage and steam until wilted. Sauté sausage. Add onion and garlic. Season to taste. Drain off any fat. Mix in cabbage, mushroom soup and cooked rice. Put in baking dish. Top with potato chips. Bake at 300°F for 30 minutes.

*8-10 servings*

# ONION BAKE THYME

| | |
|---|---|
| 2 quarts chicken broth | 4 tablespoons butter, |
| (or 2 quarts water and | melted |
| chicken bouillon cubes) | 1 teaspoon salt |
| 10 medium sized onions, | ½ teaspoon white pepper |
| peeled | ¼ teaspoon garlic powder |
| | ¾ teaspoon paprika |

**Thyme topping:**

| | |
|---|---|
| ½ cup Italian bread crumbs | 2 tablespoons butter |
| ¼ teaspoon salt | ¼ teaspoon thyme |
| ⅛ teaspoon cayenne red | |
| pepper | |

Add 2 quarts of water, chicken bouillon cubes, and peeled onions into a 6 quart saucepan. Simmer 30 minutes. Melt 3 tablespoons of butter and mix with paprika, white pepper, garlic powder and salt in small saucepan. Spread mixture on top of foil lining of baking pan. Cover each onion by brushing with the paprika mix. Align in the pan and bake uncovered, at 250°F for 10 minutes. Melt 2 tablespoons of butter in a saucepan and mix with topping ingredients. Sprinkle over onions and bake for 10 minutes more. Remove from oven and serve.

*8 servings*

**To serve as a vegetable with seafood, try adding 1 tablespoon each of celery seed and crab boil liquid when boiling onions.**

## SPANISH CONTRIBUTIONS TO CAJUN CUISINE

Shortly after their arrival in Louisiana, the Acadian exiles came into contact with Spaniards from Malaga and the Canary Islands. These transplanted Spaniards—with names like Romero, Miguez, Hernandez, Martinez, Segura, and many others—were quickly absorbed by the Acadians, but the Acadians—and their Cajun descendants—were, in turn, transformed by the people they assimilated. The use of Spanish spices in Cajun cooking is easily recognizable, but other Spanish contributions are less well known. Spaniards were largely responsible for introducing the Acadians/Cajuns to eggplants. Cajuns, for example, never refer to eggplant by its French name—*aubergine*; instead, they call it *brême*, a French corruption of *berenjena*, the Spanish term for the plant. Cajuns also call their distinctive drip coffee pots *grègues*, a French corruption of *greca*, the original Cuban-Spanish term for the pot. Spaniards also contributed red beans and rice and perhaps jambalaya as well to Louisiana. Originally considered part of the Creole culinary repertoire, red beans and rice and jambalaya have come, in this century, to constitute an integral part of the Cajun cooking tradition.

## MARINATED MUSHROOMS

**2 large jars button (whole) mushrooms**

**1½ cup Italian salad dressing**

Drain mushrooms. Place in bowl and cover with 1½ cup Italian salad dressing. Marinate overnight in refrigerator. Drain liquid. Place mushrooms in serving bowl and serve with toothpicks.

## MACARONI & CHEESE SUPREME

8 ounces elbow macaroni
3 tablespoons butter
¼ cup chopped onion
3 tablespoon flour
½ teaspoon salt
⅛ teaspoon black pepper

1 cup heavy cream
½ cup white wine or
  vermouth
2½ cup extra sharp grated
  cheddar cheese

Boil macaroni in boiling salted water according to directions. Drain. Set aside. Meanwhile melt butter, add onion, sauté till tender. Stir in flour, salt and pepper. Slowly add cream and wine. Cook over low heat, stirring till thickened. Stir cheese in until melted. Add macaroni. Pour into casserole dish. Should be thoroughly heated and cheese sauce browned and bubbly.

*4-6 servings*

## BEE'S ASPARAGUS ROLL UPS

1 pound Longhorn cheese
2 tablespoons mayonnaise
¼ teaspoon red pepper
horseradish to taste
1 loaf thin sliced fresh
  bread

round white hors d'oeuvre
  picks
1 large bell pepper chopped
  fine
1 large can green or white
  asparagus

Grate cheese and blend in mayonnaise, red pepper, and horse-radish. Remove crusts from bread and spread cheese mixture thinly on bread slices, sprinkle with finely chopped bell pepper. Roll around asparagus stalks and fasten with picks. Toast under broiler until brown. (Do not toast too slowly, as cheese melts quickly.)

*Makes 18 to 20, if used with cocktails,*
*cut in half and you will have 36 to 40 small rolls.*

## SKILLET MIRLITONS

**6-8 mirlitons**
**⅓ cup milk**
**½ cup grated cheddar
  cheese (more, if desired)**

**non-stick cooking spray**
**salt and pepper to taste**

Scrub mirlitons. Boil with skins on, about 30 minutes. Cool, peel and mash. Drain as much liquid as possible. In sprayed skillet, place mirlitons, milk, and seasonings. Cook on low heat 10-15 minutes, or until milk is almost gone. Cover with cheese and let melt. Serve in skillet or remove carefully to serving dish.

*3-4 servings*

## PASTA WITH TOMATOES AND HERBS

**1 pound ripe home grown
  tomatoes**
**4 medium garlic cloves**
**½ cup virgin olive oil**

**20 or so large basil leaves**
**1 pound dried shell pasta**
**salt and fresh ground
  pepper**

Wash tomatoes and cut them into small pieces and put in bowl. Chop garlic coarsely, add to bowl. Tear basil leaves into small pieces and add to bowl along with olive oil. Salt and fresh ground pepper to taste. Mix all ingredients together, then cover bowl and place in refrigerator for about two hours before serving time. When ready to serve, put large amount of salted water in pot and set on high heat. Cook pasta according to directions on package. Drain quickly and place in a large serving bowl. While the pasta is still very hot, combine the refrigerated sauce with the pasta and toss well. Serve at once as it is the reaction of cold with hot that releases the unique flavor of this dish.

*4 servings*

Cajuns speak their mind, but sometimes they have a colorful way of putting things that might be confusing to others:

"Two neighbors were discussing the sale of a mule by one to the other. 'Arceneaux, now don't you try to talk me out of buying your mule,' said Leblanc. 'You say he don't look so good, but to me he looks very good. He's got strong legs, a big chest and his tail...well it hangs over his rear end just right.' 'OK Leblanc, you win,' answered Arceneaux, 'I will sold him to you for $200 because we are such good frands.' Leblanc loaded the mule into his trailer and took off for his farm. Two days later he hurriedly drove his truck back to the gate of Arceneaux's farm with the mule loaded in the trailer. 'Doggone you Arceneaux,' hollered Leblanc, 'I never taught you would pull a stunt like dat on me. Dat mule, he's blind in both eyes!' Arceneaux looked calmly at his angry friend, 'Mais what stunt I pulled on you. I told you in the first place dat mule don't look so good, hanh!'"

## ARTICHOKE HEARTS CASSEROLE

4 cans (not jars) artichoke hearts, drained
6 pods garlic
grated Italian cheese, bread crumbs and olive oil to cover each layer

⅛ inch water or liquid from artichokes
salt and pepper to taste

Place water in bottom of casserole. Place half the artichokes in dish and cover with half the garlic. Sprinkle bread crumbs and cheese to cover. Drizzle olive oil until saturated. Repeat layers. Add seasoning to taste. Bake at 350°F for 45 minutes.

*4-6 servings*

# LOTE "GOAT"

The December 1976 issue of *La Gazette des Acadiens*, a Jennings, Louisiana, newspaper, carried an article by Peggy Mengis of Opelousas. Mengis wrote about Lote Thistlethwaite, a colorful Cajun who, even today, depicts the typical self-made Cajun cook. Lost as a reserve pilot during the Korean Conflict, Thistlethwaite's legend as a compassionate, fun-loving master chef lives on. Lote was called "goat" by his friends. He loved to hunt, fish, and concoct tantalizing dishes with his catch.

Lote wasn't one to measure. He cooked instinctively, adding a handful of this and a pinch of that, and the finished product defied description. His zest for living translated into his culinary creations.

He started his recipe for court-bouillon, a rich, savory fish stew, with the usual "first you make a roux" procedure. Heat three or four tablespoons of flour in the same amount of vegetable oils. Brown flour and then add three or four onions, two or three cloves of garlic, four stalks of celery, a green pepper, some green onion, and some parsley, all chopped fine. Cook until the mixture is limp-limp. Add a can of mashed tomatoes (tomato paste), and then a can of tomato sauce. Add some water, then Tabasco, salt, and red pepper, and one-third bottle of Worcestershire sauce, and a pinch of thyme. Add the juice of one-third lemon. Let the mixture cook down and about a half-hour before serving, add the fish. "Catfish is good," Lote said. Other recipes call for redfish, but Lote used whatever he happened to catch.

When asked to explain the difference between "limp" and "limp-limp," he retorted, "Well, Cher, if you don't know the difference between 'limp' and 'limp-limp' [which he pronounced 'lamp'], you shouldn't be trying to cook!"

Lote's recipe for sauce piquante was short and simple: "Same as court-bouillon, except thick-thick." (He wasn't asked to explain the difference between "thick" and "thick-thick.")

Any wild game killed on hunting trips was put into a sauce piquante. Listening to the tales of the savory stews cooked in the woods by hunters at the end of the day was enough to make your mouth water. Imagine the aroma arising from a quail, or squirrel, or rabbit sauce piquante.

Lote also made bouillabaisse. Lote would fillet a large fish. Catfish was his favorite ingredient for bouillabaisse, too. After you fillet the fish, take the bones and boil them, and save the stock. Take an onion, cut it into four pieces and put them into the water with thyme, parsley, garlic and two bay leaves. Mix salt, red pepper, thyme, broken bay leaves, and chopped parsley and rub these seasonings into the fish fillets.

Chop up three onions, three onion tops, celery, green pepper, and garlic. Brown the chopped vegetables in three tablespoons of olive oil.

Add fish. Cook five minutes on each side.

You can add a few shrimp. After cooking add the fish stock to the sauce and add a can of mashed tomatoes and one pint of white port wine. Cook down some, then return the fish to the pot. Cover and cook about twenty minutes longer.

In the meantime, fry bread in oleo, put fish on top of the bread, cover the fish with sauce, and eat. "And that is good-good, Cher."

# Cajun MEN COOK SEAFOOD

OYSTERS

# SEAFOOD

# BAKED SHRIMP

2 sticks margarine
1½ tablespoons liquid crab
  boil
½ teaspoon red pepper
½ teaspoon black pepper

juice of 2 lemons
½ teaspoon oregano
dash garlic salt
5 pounds medium shrimp,
  raw unpeeled

On top of stove, in broiler pan, melt margarine; add all ingredients except shrimp. Simmer 5 minutes. Heat oven to 350°F. Add washed shrimp to broiler pan and transfer to oven. Bake 10 minutes. Stir well and bake additional 10 minutes. When serving, place in soup bowls with butter sauce spooned over shrimp. Provide lots of French bread for dunking in sauce. Very messy, but, oh, so good.

*4-6 servings*

# MARDI GRAS SHRIMP

1 pound peeled raw shrimp
1 tablespoon oleo
1 tablespoon oil
1 small onion, chopped
½ green bell pepper,
  chopped
½ red bell pepper, chopped
½ yellow bell pepper,
  chopped

1 tablespoon Louisiana
  Cane Syrup
1 tablespoon dry sherry
1 teaspoon Worcestershire
  sauce
1 teaspoon hot sauce, salt
  and cracked black pepper
  to taste
¼ cup of chopped parsley

Sauté shrimp until pink in combined oleo and oil. Sauté onions and bell peppers. Add all other ingredients. Garnish with parsley. Good over noodles.

*4 servings*

*A little finely shredded purple cabbage sprinkled on top of dish will complete the Mardi Gras royal colors.*

## BACON WRAPPED SHRIMP

**3 pounds peeled shrimp**
**½ cup chopped green**
**  onions**
**garlic salt to taste**

**1 pound bacon (cut strips in**
**  half)**
**½ stick butter**
**1 cup Worcestershire sauce**
**Creole seasoning**

In a large bowl, mix shrimp, green onions, garlic salt, and Worcestershire sauce. Marinate for 20 minutes. Wrap bacon strips around individual shrimp and insert toothpick to hold bacon in place. Place bacon-wrapped shrimp in glass dish, add ½ stick of butter and remainder of shrimp mixture (marinade sauce). Bake at 350°F for 15-20 minutes.

## COSMOPOLITAN ACADIANA

Acadiana is the most cosmopolitan area of the upper Gulf Coast—with the exception of New Orleans. Acadiana has historically provided a haven to refugees from both the new and the old worlds. At least sixteen French-speaking groups settled in the region in the eighteenth and nineteenth centuries. These immigrants were joined by Canary Islanders, Malagueños from southern Spain, Africans, West Indies refugees, Irishmen, Germans, Italians, Cubans, Vietnamese, and many others. Acadiana's premier university—the University of Southwestern Louisiana at Lafayette— is also home to hundreds of international students. The result has been a cosmopolitan atmosphere found in few places in the United States. This is seen perhaps most clearly in Lafayette's Festival Internationale, and, not surprisingly, in the eclectic collection of the following recipes.

# SHRIMP AND HAM JAMBALAYA

1½ cup vegetable oil
1 teaspoon thyme
2 teaspoons salt
¼ teaspoon white pepper
½ teaspoon red pepper
½ teaspoon black pepper
1 teaspoon dry sweet basil
  or 1 tablespoon fresh basil
1 tablespoon sugar
5-6 bay leaves
3 pods fresh garlic, chopped
3 large onions, finely
  chopped
2 large bell peppers, finely
  chopped

3 ribs celery, finely
  chopped
6 pounds fresh tomatoes,
  cored, peeled and mashed,
  or 2 14 ounce cans whole
  tomatoes same way
1 pound ham, chopped
4 ounces tomato sauce
2 pounds fresh small
  shrimp (60-70 count)
  cleaned and deveined
2 cups chopped green
  onions
1 cup chopped parsley
2 cups uncooked rice,
  cooked

Mix first seven ingredients in a bowl. In a large Dutch oven, sauté onions, bell peppers, garlic and celery in oil over medium high temperature stirring often for 45 minutes. Add all seasonings from bowl. Add the next ingredients through tomato sauce. Let cook for at least 1½ - 2 hours. You can prepare 2-3 days before serving. Refrigerate well. This is a stopping point if prepared ahead of time. Then add shrimp, let cook over medium fire 4-5 minutes or until pink. Once again remember: the more you cook seafood, the more flavor you cook out of it. Add cut green onions and parsley. In a separate bowl, mix Jambalaya and uncooked rice which has been cooked.

*6-8 servings*

## SHRIMP AND PORK JAMBALAYA

2 pounds pork finger, cubed
1 pound smoked pork
  sausage, cut into ¼ inch
  slices
½ cup cooking oil
1 cup water
1 cup cooked ham, cubed
1 cup medium shrimp,
  peeled and deveined
1 cup onions, chopped
1 ribs celery, chopped
5 cloves garlic, chopped
1 small bell pepper,
  chopped

1 cup water
1 teaspoon browning and
  seasoning sauce
3 cups rice
1½ teaspoon salt
½ teaspoon fresh ground
  black pepper
⅛ teaspoon cayenne red
  pepper
2 cups water
3 sprigs parsley, chopped
6 leaves of onion tops,
  chopped

Heat oil in a 4 quart iron pot. Add sausage; brown, uncovered, on a medium fire-about 10 minutes. Remove; add pork meat and brown about 10 minutes. Add garlic, onion, celery, and bell pepper; sauté, covered, until onion is opaque, about 5 minutes. Add 1 cup of water, cover, and simmer for 25 minutes. Add all other ingredients except onion tops and parsley and 2 more cups of water; cover and simmer for 30 minutes or until rice is done. Stir pot only once with rice added. Add onion tops and parsley while fluffing rice after it is cooked. Cover and let stand 5 minutes before serving.

*6 servings*

# SHRIMP SCAMPI

¼ cup butter
¼ cup olive oil
4-6 tablespoons chopped
  parsley
1 tablespoon garlic powder
½ teaspoon salt

dash cayenne
2 tablespoons fresh lemon
  juice
1 pound shrimp, peeled,
  deveined (tails left on)

Preheat oven to 400°F. In large skillet (that can be put in oven) melt butter, oil, 3-4 tablespoons parsley, garlic powder, salt, cayenne, and lemon juice; mix well and add shrimp, toss to coat, and arrange in single layer. Bake in oven 8-10 minutes, or just until tender. Garnish with remaining parsley and lemon slice. Serve shrimp in shallow bowl with plain French bread for "dipping" into sauce.

*2 servings*

# NEW ORLEANS QUE SHRIMP

2 pounds fresh shrimp,
  unpeeled with heads,
  preferred
3 ounces spicy seafood
  sauce
¼ teaspoon hot pepper
  sauce
1 tablespoon garlic powder
1 teaspoon black pepper,
  chopped fine
½ lemon, juice

1 medium onion, finely
  chopped
½ medium bell pepper,
  chopped fine
1½ teaspoon salt
2 sticks butter
1 tablespoon Worcestershire
  sauce
2 tablespoons fresh parsley,
  finely chopped

Wash and drain shrimp. Sauté all vegetables in skillet of melted butter until onion is opaque, about 10 minutes at medium heat. Add seasoning, mixing thoroughly. Place shrimp into baking pan and pour and mix sauce. Bake at 350°F for 12 minutes. Stir as needed to keep shrimp moist with sauce.

*4 servings*

## SHRIMP/FISH PAN BRAISE

2 pounds 20/30 count fresh
or frozen shrimp, peeled
and deveined, or your
favorite fish fillet
½ cup fresh parsley,
chopped
1½ sticks butter

½ teaspoon cayenne pepper
½ teaspoon garlic salt
½ teaspoon garlic powder
½ teaspoon salt
½ teaspoon basil, ground
½ teaspoon white pepper
1 lemon, juice

Mix dry seasonings together. Set aside. Melt butter in skillet and add parsley. Set aside half of mixture. Heat mix until fry hot. Place ½ of shrimp or ½ of fish in hot skillet. Brown on each side, sprinkling seasoning and lemon juice on each side during browning. (Use about half of seasoning). Remove when golden brown (not blackened), about 6 minutes. Add second batch of oil, parsley and fish and repeat the process.

*6 servings*

*Two batches give better control of browning.*

*This is a very quick and easy recipe to prepare and can be used to braise-fry fish, shrimp, alligator, lobster, or even crawfish tails. Serve with stuffed baked potatoes, broccoli, a tossed salad and toasted garlic bread.*

## SHRIMP AND ZUCCHINI FETTUCCINE

¼ pound butter
3 tablespoons flour
1 medium onion
1 tablespoon garlic
1 pound fettuccine
½ pint whipping cream (or 1
can evaporated milk)
1 cup Parmesan cheese (can
add more if it needs it,
may add yellow cheese)

¼ cup dried parsley (or 1
cup fresh parsley)
2 small zucchini (cut into
thin "match sticks")
2 tablespoons salt
2 tablespoons pepper
1 pound shrimp

Melt butter. Add flour and blend. Add onion salt, pepper, garlic, parsley, and zucchini. Cook on medium fire for 15 minutes, stirring frequently. Add shrimp. Cook fettuccine. Add cream to shrimp and simmer until shrimp are cooked. Mix together. Add green onions and Parmesan cheese.

# WOK SHRIMP/GARLIC PASTA

1 pound fresh medium
  shrimp, deveined
3 sprigs green onions,
  chopped fine
8 cloves garlic, chopped
  fine
8 fresh mushrooms,
  chopped fine
2 tablespoons olive oil
½ teaspoon liquid smoke
⅛ teaspoon cayenne red
  pepper

1 12 ounce package elbow
  noodles, or your choice
1 tablespoon corn starch
½ teaspoon garlic powder
½ teaspoon Chinese spices
1 teaspoon 4 herb
  seasonings of equal mix of
  thyme, tarragon, basil and
  oregano
½ cup water
teriyaki sauce

Using a 2 quart wok: boil noodles, drain and set aside. Marinate shrimp with oil, Teriyaki, garlic powder, Chinese spices, 4 season mix and liquid smoke. Refrigerate until ready to use. Coat wok with oil and heat until hot. Add shrimp and marinade sauce. Stir fry until shrimp is whitish in color, about 3 minutes. Remove shrimp and set aside. Re-coat wok with oil; get hot. Add and then stir fry all vegetables until wilted but not browned, about 3 minutes. Dissolve corn starch in water. Slowly add to vegetables. Add marinade juices and shrimp. Remove from heat; add pasta. Adjust seasonings. Add a little more water, if needed. Serve while hot.

*4 servings*

# DE SHRIMP BOAT

8 French style dinner buns
½ stick corn oil margarine
2 pounds small shrimp,
  peeled and deveined
½ cup canned mushroom
  stems and pieces
¼ teaspoon dried Italian
  seasoning
2 tablespoons white onion,
  coarsely chopped

pinch oregano
4 tablespoons mayonnaise
1 cup shredded mozzarella
  cheese
½ cup black olives, coarsely
  chopped
1 cup fresh diced tomatoes
1 cup shredded lettuce

Lightly toast buns in oven at 350°F. Cut one inch wide wedge cut at a 45 degree angle half depth of the bun. Set wedges and rolls aside. Melt margarine in skillet and sauté shrimp, mushrooms, adding Italian seasoning, onions, and oregano. Cook only till the shrimp is light pink, about 3 minutes on medium heat. Remove from fire and let cool. Then add mayonnaise and mozzarella cheese. Be sure it is cooled so as not to melt the cheese at this point. Put rolls on an ungreased pizza tin. Spoon generous helpings of sautéed shrimp mixture. Put in oven and bake at 350°F until cheese is bubbly — approximately 5 minutes. Serve open-faced. Sprinkle olive, tomatoes and lettuce over each boat. Use wedges as a sopping bread or place on top of boat.

*6 servings*

# CRAWFISH PIE

2 pounds peeled crawfish
1 teaspoon garlic powder
  (seasoned)
1½ cup tap water
½ cup cooking oil
parsley and onion tops

½ cup flour
hot sauce to taste
2 chopped onions
1 pie shell
½ bell pepper

Cook uncovered. Make a light colored roux; add onions and bell pepper until wilted. Add water, garlic and well seasoned crawfish tails. Cook uncovered until crawfish are tender, but firm. Add parsley and onion tops. Fill pie shells and bake at 375°F for 30 minutes.

*6-8 servings*

# CRAWFISH IN SQUASH PIROGUE

2 medium yellow squash
¼ teaspoon each of basil,
  thyme, and rosemary
1 pound crawfish meat
½ stick butter
1 teaspoon hot pepper
  sauce
1 large onion, chopped fine
¾ cup Italian seasoned
  bread crumbs
1 pound fresh mushrooms,
  sliced
½ cup dry white wine
4 ounces fresh Parmesan,
  grated
juice of 1 lemon
cheese, grate
1 teaspoon salt
1 10½ ounce can cream of
  celery soup
½ teaspoon black pepper
⅛ teaspoon cayenne red
  pepper
¼ cup half-n-half cream
1 teaspoon garlic powder
4 tablespoons butter

Boil squash, covered, in one quart of salt water. (Two teaspoons of salt). Cook for 10 minutes on medium heat. Drain and set aside to cool. Cut squash lengthwise and scoop out the pulp. Set pulp aside and put shells in a 8x8x2 inch greased baking dish. Add vegetables, except mushrooms, into a 2 quart sauce pan and sauté in melted butter on low heat until onion is opaque, about 10 minutes. Add crawfish and wine. Simmer, uncovered, for 5 minutes. Remove crawfish and set aside. Add squash pulp, lemon juice, seasonings and pepper sauce. Stir on low fire until water evaporates, about 15 minutes. Add crawfish, half of the bread crumbs, and grated cheese. Blend in soup and cream with squash mixture. Remove from heat. Stuff the four squash ½ shells with the stuffing. Top with remaining crumbs and margarine. Bake at 350°F for 30 minutes.

*4 servings*

# CRAWFISH BROCCOLI CASSEROLE

2 stalks celery, chopped
3 tablespoons butter or oleo
1½ cup cooked rice, no salt
1 soup can of milk
1 box frozen broccoli spears
1 small jar jalapeño cheese
  spread

1 can whole kernel corn
1 can cream of chicken
  soup
2 pounds crawfish
1 cup onion, chopped

Bring cup of water to boil. Put in broccoli to thaw; drain. Sauté onion and celery in butter. Add soup and milk and mix. Then add cheese spread. Simmer for a few minutes. Add broccoli. Place in baking dish. Bake 20 minutes at 350°F, uncovered. Add crawfish tails. Then cover and bake for 20 more minutes.

*6-8 servings*

# CRAWFISH FETTUCINE

½ cup of margarine
⅔ teaspoon jalapeño relish
1 medium onion, finely
  chopped
⅔ clove garlic, minced
1 small bell pepper, finely
  chopped
salt, red and black pepper
  to taste
¹⁄₁₆ cup all-purpose flour

1½ tablespoon dehydrated
  parsley
1 pound fine fettucine
  noodles, cooked
1 pound crawfish tails,
  peeled
⅓ cup Half and Half cream
Parmesan cheese for
  sprinkling
6 ounces pasteurized
  process cheese spread

Melt margarine in a large saucepan. Add onions and bell pepper. Cook covered until tender, approximately 15-20 minutes. Add flour. Cover and cook approximately 15 minutes, stirring frequently to prevent sticking. Add parsley and crawfish tails. Cook covered 15 minutes, stirring frequently. Add cream, cheese, jalapeño relish, garlic, salt and pepper. Cover and cook on low heat 30 minutes, stirring occasionally. Cook fettucine according to package directions. Mix crawfish mixture and fettucine noodles thoroughly. Pour mixture into casserole. Sprinkle top with Parmesan cheese. Bake in preheated oven 15-20 minutes until heated through.

# "CAMP STYLE" RECIPES

A restaurant on the edge of the great Atchafalaya Basin serves two varieties of crawfish étouffée—regular and "camp style." When asked about the difference (other than the slightly higher price for "camp style"), the waitress said, in a thick Cajun accent: "You know those Cajun men. When they go to their fishing camps, they stay up late playing cards and drink too much. When it comes time to cook they're tired and not in much shape to cook. When they chop up the onions, bell peppers, and celery for the étouffée, they don't do too good of a job of chopping." Sure enough, when the "camp style" étouffée was served, there were large, uneven chunks of onions, bell peppers, and celery, as opposed to the finely chopped ingredients of the other variety. It was delicious and somehow "camp style" has a slightly better flavor, perhaps induced by thoughts of a group of friends, together in the wilderness, cooking for the pleasure of it.

## CRAWFISH ÉTOUFFÉE

2 pounds crawfish
1 teaspoon cayenne pepper
1 large onion
1 cup hot water
¼ cup cooking oil

1 can cream of mushroom
soup (or 2 cups of crawfish
fat)
1 cup shallots
2 tablespoons parsley
2 teaspoons salt

In a large saucepan, add oil, heat, then add onions. Sauté 2 to 4 minutes, add crawfish, cook 15 minutes. Add crawfish fat or cream of mushroom soup; cook 10 minutes. Keep stirring because it will stick; add water, lower heat to low. Add shallots and parsley; cook 2 to 3 minutes, taste and season. Add more seasoning if necessary. Serve over hot rice.

## HEART-LOVING CRAWFISH ÉTOUFFÉE

1 pound crawfish tails
2 stalks celery, chopped
1 large onion, chopped
1 pack instant potatoes
2 cloves garlic, minced

salt and red pepper to taste
1 bell pepper, chopped
1 heaping teaspoon corn
starch

Spray fry pan with non-stick spray and sauté all vegetables until soft. Add potatoes mixed according to package directions. Add crawfish, salt, red pepper, and corn starch mix with ¼ cup water. Cover and simmer 15 minutes until gravy is of desired consistency. Serve over rice. You'll never know that it is health food!

## CRAWFISH MAQUE CHOUX

1 pound cleaned crawfish
tails (seasoned)
1 can cream style corn
1 stick butter

1 can tomatoes with chiles
1 onion, chopped
1 can whole kernel corn
½ green pepper, chopped

Sauté onion and pepper in butter. Drain tomatoes and sauté until purée. Add whole kernel corn; cook until corn is tender. Add cream style and crawfish; cook 20 minutes.

# CRAWFISH STEW

4 onions, chopped fine
½ cup margarine
3 ribs celery, chopped fine
3 pounds crawfish tails
⅓ cup flour
3 cups crawfish fat
1 pound butter
5 cups water
5-6 drops hot sauce

1 cup fresh parsley, chopped
1 cup green onions, chopped
salt and black pepper to taste (with a little red pepper)
3 bell peppers, chopped fine

First make the roux; melt ½ cup of margarine and stir in ⅓ cup of flour. Cook slowly over low heat, stirring often, until the color of peanut butter. The color is vital; make sure it is a golden brown and not too dark. Set aside. Melt 1 pound of butter in a large skillet and add the mixed peppers, onions and celery. Sauté over high heat, stirring often, for 30-45 minutes. Add the roux. Thoroughly stir onto vegetables, making certain all is well mixed, evenly colored, and no oil floating on top or at sides of dish. If oil begins to separate, simply keep stirring mix well and simmer over high heat for about 10 minutes. Season with salt, pepper and hot sauce. Let simmer 5 minutes, stirring occasionally to keep from sticking or separating. Meanwhile, pour tails into large bowl and wash in about 5 cups of water. When thoroughly rinsed, pour water into sauce. Stir and cook 10-15 minutes. Add crawfish tails and simmer another 5-10 minutes until flavors blend and sauce is slightly thickened. Top with green onion tops and parsley and serve in bowls over rice.

*10 servings*

# CRAWFISH PIZZA

1 tablespoon olive oil
1 loaf Italian-style bread
¼ bunch green onions, chopped
1 pound crawfish tails
1½ cups bottled tomato sauce

1 pound mozzarella cheese, grated (or substitute your own)
½ tablespoon garlic salt
6 tablespoons Parmesan cheese
1 tablespoon dried oregano

Sauté green onions in olive oil until wilted; stir in tomato sauce and garlic salt. Spread sauce on Italian-style bread loaf which has been split in two lengthwise. Top with crawfish tails. Sprinkle cheeses and dried oregano on top of crawfish. Bake at 350°F about 20 minutes or until cheeses melt and bubble. Make one loaf split in two halves.

# CRABMEAT MORNAY

1 stick butter or oleo
2 tablespoons flour
1 pint breakfast cream (or Half & Half)
½ pound grated Swiss cheese
½ clove garlic, minced
2 tablespoons of minced parsley

2 tablespoons dry white wine
4 green onions, chopped
1 pound lump crabmeat
salt, black, red pepper to taste

Sauté green onions, parsley and garlic in butter until the onions are limp only (do not brown) for approximately 10 minutes. Add flour. Blend well and then gradually add cream until the sauce is creamy. Add cheese, wine and seasonings. Fold in the crabmeat and simmer for 2 minutes. Serve immediately!

*4 servings*

*This is a choice dish for a romantic "stay at home," entrée complemented by candlelight, a good white wine, and of course your "Sha-T-BéBé." Serve with a spinach salad, creamed potatoes, green peas, and garlic French bread. Watch the wine intake — might get you in trouble!*

# FISHERMAN CRAB STEW

6 large fat crabs (or 1 dozen
small and thin crabs)
3 cups beef stock
2 beef bouillon cubes
4 tablespoons bacon fat or
oil dissolved in 3 cups of
water)
3 medium onions, chopped
4 cloves garlic, chopped
1 pound crabmeat
1 large bell pepper, chopped

¼ teaspoon chili powder
3 ribs celery, chopped
3 bay leaves
6 green onions, chopped
¼ teaspoon chili powder
6 sprigs parsley, chopped
1 tablespoon Worcestershire
sauce
4 tablespoons flour
salt and pepper to taste

Clean crabs by washing, and removing claws, gills, apron, and shells from the body. Also remove swimmerettes. Cut body segment in half. Melt fat or oil over a low heat. Add onions, garlic, bell pepper, and celery and simmer for 10 minutes or until light brown. Stir in flour and stir until brown. About 10 minutes. Add beef stock, crabmeat, bay leaf, chili powder, thyme and then simmer slowly for 30 minutes. Stir as needed. Add parsley, green onions, Worcestershire sauce, salt and pepper. Stir for 3 minutes and let set for 10 minutes. Serve over fluffy rice. Note: If desire to be thicker mix two tablespoons of cornstarch with 2 cups of water and add when last ingredients are placed in stew.

*6 servings*

*To tell if a crab is thin look at the body. If translucent with bluish tinge, it is usually empty. If light brown creamy opaque, it is usually full. Be sure crab is clean when you look as you can be fooled if they need a bath, Yea!*

# T-BOY STUFFED CRAB

3 cups crabmeat
¾ cup light cream
1 large onion, minced
3 hard boiled eggs
6 stalks green onion,
  minced
1½ tablespoons sherry
2 tablespoons parsley,
  minced
⅛ teaspoon red pepper
1½ stick butter
¼ teaspoon pepper sauce
¾ cup seasoned bread
  crumbs
⅛ teaspoon powdered
  thyme
juice of 1½ lemons
salt and black pepper to
  taste
12 medium crab shells,
  cleaned

Melt ¾ stick of butter in pot and add onions and green onions. On low fire sauté for 10 minutes until opaque. Do not brown. Add the bread crumbs and mix well. Next add parsley, eggs, crabmeat, cream and sherry. Mix well. Be sure the crabmeat is well distributed throughout the mix. Season with pepper sauce, red pepper, salt, black pepper and thyme. Stir and let sit off the fire. Butter lightly the inside of crab shells. Fill with mix. Sprinkle stuffed shells with seasoned bread crumbs. Melt butter and spread approximately 1 teaspoon on top of each stuffed crab. Bake in a 375°F oven until tops start to slightly brown.

*6 servings*

# BLUE POINT CRAB PATTIES

1 pound fresh lump crab (or fresh frozen)
1 tablespoon corn starch
½ stick oleo or butter
4 celery ribs, finely chopped
¼ teaspoon ground nutmeg or mace
6 green onions, finely chopped
1 cup bread crumbs
¼ teaspoon thyme

2 hard boiled eggs, finely chopped
¼ teaspoon hot pepper sauce
1 10½ ounce can beef consommé
dash of Allspice, cloves
⅛ teaspoon black pepper
3 tablespoons cooking oil
¼ teaspoon salt
flour

Sauté onions and celery in hot cooking oil on medium heat in heavy iron pot until opaque. Add all seasonings except crumbs, consommé, eggs, corn starch, and crabmeat. Moisten the cup of bread crumbs with part of the consommé, to the texture of a pie crust. Save excess consommé for another dish. Mix well with vegetables. Lower the heat and add crabmeat, chopped eggs, and corn starch and stir well. Remove mixture from the pot and make into crab patties approximately 2x¾ inch thick. Coat each patty with flour. Heat butter and cooking oil in a heavy iron pot and fry each crab patty until well browned and crisp. Set patties to drain on cookie tray lined with a brown paper bag.

*6 servings*

## CRABMEAT IMPERIAL

1 pound lump crabmeat
½ teaspoon dry mustard
½ medium size onion,
  chopped fine
½ teaspoon salt
1½ cups half-n-half cream
2 teaspoons minced chives

¾ stick butter (not
  margarine) (frozen)
3 tablespoons flour
hot sauce and Creole
  seasoning, to taste
2 egg yolks, slightly beaten

Melt butter in saucepan. Add onion and sauté 10 minutes. Add crabmeat. Cook on low for 5 minutes. Add flour and stir until well mixed. Add half-n-half gradually and continue stirring until mixture boils. Mix mustard, salt and chives with egg yolks. Add small amount of hot crab mixture to yolk mixture. Then add this back to the crabmeat mixture. Season to taste with hot sauce and Creole seasoning. Serve this in a chafing dish with crackers.

*This is also wonderful in pastry shells or as a casserole with bread crumbs on top and baked in a 350°F oven for 20 minutes until bubbly and golden.*

# CORN AND CRAB MAQUE CHOUX

2 pounds freshly peeled
crabmeat (or crawfish tails
or shrimp)
3 medium onions, chopped
2 bell peppers, chopped
2 sticks margarine

6 roasting ears corn or 2
cans of whole kernel corn
1 can tomatoes with green
chilies
salt, pepper and garlic to
taste
parsley and onion tips

Place chopped onions and bell peppers in a 1 quart saucepan and sauté with 2 sticks of margarine. Cook about 15 minutes, stirring occasionally, over medium heat. Then add fresh corn cut from 6 roasting ears or 2 cans of whole kernel corn. Add 1 can of tomatoes with green chilies, salt, pepper and garlic to taste. Stir well. Cook over medium heat until corn is tender, or approximately 1 hour, stirring occasionally. Then add 2 pounds of crabmeat, (or crawfish tails or shrimp) stir well and cook over medium heat for 20 minutes. Now time is drawing near for the taste treat of your life. Turn off heat and add fresh cut parsley and onion tips. Stir well, let rest for 8 minutes or so, and enjoy.

# STUFFED CATFISH

2 pounds fillet catfish (or
four large fillets)
2 8 ounce packages cream
cheese
1 pound crawfish tails

¼ teaspoon dry parsley
1 stick butter
¼ teaspoon red pepper
1 cup green onions
1 cup onion tops

Season fillets to taste, (salt, pepper, garlic powder, etc.). Broil at 500°F on pan lined with foil and sprayed with non-stick spray until golden brown. Melt butter in skillet, add green onions. Sauté 5 minutes. Add crawfish and simmer for 10 minutes. Melt cream cheese in crawfish mix and cook until bubbly (approximately 5 minutes). Add other seasonings. Spoon over catfish fillet and serve.

*4 servings*

# OYSTERS

Cajuns are experts at using foods readily available to them. Louisiana, with its many miles of coastal bays, bayous, and rivers, has long been noted for its delicious oysters. Through the efforts of the State Department of Wildlife and Fisheries, oyster "farming" has become an important Louisiana industry. Empty oyster shells are collected and returned to the water in "bedding" areas, where newly hatched mollusks attach and begin growing. Since oysters filter surrounding water for food (about five gallons per day), pollution is closely monitored in the bed areas. Before the advent of modern refrigeration, oysters were usually harvested only in the winter months. Though an old wives' tale maintained that oysters should only be eaten in months that contained the letter "R"—the cooler months from September through April, Louisiana oysters are available year-round. Louisiana oysters are eaten raw on the half-shell, deep fried in a cornmeal batter, made into oyster soup and stews, or, most commonly, cooked in gumbos, dressings, and stuffings. An avid raw oyster lover can easily consume a dozen or so mollusks at a sitting, usually dunking them into a spicy sauce made of lemon juice, catsup, hot pepper sauce, Worcestershire sauce, and often horseradish. The ratio of ingredients varies according to each oyster lover's taste. New Orleans has hundreds of oyster bars, where patrons stand at tall counters consuming the tasty mollusks, served by the dozen or half-dozen on round trays with a sauce bowl located in the center. Fresh crackers are always served with the oysters and ice-cold beer is usually the beverage of choice.

You may have heard that raw oysters are considered aphrodisiacs. Most oyster fans will tell you that after consuming a dozen or more oysters, the only thing on your mind is a nap!

# ELLENDER'S OYSTER JAMBALAYA

**Basic Sauce:**

5 tablespoons fat (vegetable or bacon fat)
1 lemon (grate rind, remove white pulpy membrane and chop rest of lemon)
1 tablespoon flour, rounded
2 pounds onions, chopped fine

a few dashes Worcestershire, hot sauce, thyme, seasoned salt
3 stalks celery, chopped fine
1 medium bell pepper, chopped fine
2 bay leaves
salt to taste

To the fat add flour and brown, stirring constantly, to make scorchy - tasting roux. Add the onions, fry slowly until well-browned and reduced to a pulp. Add rest of the ingredients at one time and continue to cook slowly for at least 30 to 45 minutes.

**Jambalaya:**

½ can tomato sauce (not paste or whole tomatoes)
¼ cup each onion tops and parsley mixed together

3 cups raw rice
3 pints oyster

Add tomato sauce to basic sauce and simmer for approximately 45 minutes; stir and add little water if needed to keep from sticking. Add oysters and simmer for 10 minutes after boiling starts. Add rice and green onion and parsley mix. Add water to assure 6 cups of rice. Adjust salt seasoning, bring to a boil, stir. Cover pot and lower fire and simmer for 25 minutes. Do not remove lid. Test rice for done-ness after 25 minutes. If not cooked, cover and simmer a little longer.

*8 servings*

# BAR-B-Q SPECKLED TROUT FILLETS

5 pounds speckled trout
  fillets
5 pounds charcoal
salt, red pepper and black
  pepper to taste

2 sticks butter
4 lemons
dash Worcestershire sauce

Preheat your Bar-B-Q pit until the flame is gone, and coals are white hot. Cover grill with aluminum foil and lower it close as possible to the coals (approximately 4 inches away.) Season the fish fillet with salt, red pepper and black pepper to taste. Put on the grill and baste with butter, lemon juice and Worcestershire sauce, being careful not to let it stick or burn. Punch approximately 4 to 6 holes in the aluminum foil to let only small amount of butter sauce drip on to the coals. This causes the meat to have a smoke taste. Fillets should take approximately 15 to 20 minutes to cook. You can check fish to see if it is done. The meat should be firm and white.

*6 to 10 servings*

# BASIN FISH FRY À LA SKERRETT

10 bass fillets
2 cups cracker meal
2 teaspoons salt
1 large onion, diced for
  frying

1 teaspoon lemon pepper
vegetable oil for frying
½ teaspoon cayenne red
  pepper

Mix seasonings together in a small bowl; be sure fillets are moist but not wet; season both sides of the fillet, rubbing into the meat gently. Put cracker meal into a brown paper bag along with fillets. Shake to coat fillets with meal. Put enough oil in a cast iron frying pan to depth approximately half the average thickness of the fillets. Heat oil until 360°F or until a fleshy onion piece will curl up as it floats on the surface of the oil. Add fillets and fry on one side until golden brown. When fillets are turned over to fry the other side, add the onions over the fish. When fish is done, remove with onions and place on a platter covered with a brown paper bag. Adjust seasoning, if needed, and serve immediately.

*4 servings*

**Try with fried potatoes and a fresh green salad.**

# CATFISH À LA ALLEN

2 pounds catfish fillets, cut
   into chunks and seasoned
   with 2 tablespoons
   prepared roux
1 10 ounce can tomatoes
   with chilies, undrained
   and blended
salt, lemon pepper, coarse
   black pepper and cayenne
   pepper

½ cup butter or margarine
1 8 ounce can tomato sauce
1 large onion, chopped
1½ cup chicken broth
½ bell pepper, chopped
¼ cup red wine
3 toes garlic, minced
1 bay leaf
⅓ cup each, parsley and
   green onion tops, chopped

Season fish and chill for two hours. Melt butter and add vegetables. Sauté 30 minutes. Add tomatoes, roux and bay leaf and cook 15-20 minutes. Add stock and wine; cover and simmer 45 minutes. Add fish and simmer 30 minutes, adding parsley and onion tops the last 10 minutes.

*Great for the hunters' camp!*

## REDFISH COURTBOUILLON

1 5 pound redfish scaled/gutted with head on
2 cloves garlic, finely chopped
1 cup peanut oil
1 cup water
½ cup flour
1 6 ounce can tomato paste
2 large onions, finely chopped
1 small bell pepper, finely chopped
½ 5 ounce can tomatoes with chiles

3 stalks celery, finely chopped
2 tablespoons Worcestershire sauce
1 tablespoon sugar
1 small bunch onion tops, finely chopped
4 whole lemons
salt, red pepper, and black pepper to taste
1 small bunch parsley, finely chopped
6 bay leaves

Filet red fish leaving skin and cut into 3 inch strips. Season with red pepper, black pepper and salt to taste and set aside.

Take the bones including the head and boil in a large skillet with 2 tablespoons of oil, 2 cups of water for about an hour. Remove deboned meat and pour stock through strainer and set aside.

Pour the remainder of your peanut oil, chopped onions, celery, bell peppers, and sauté for about 30 minutes (until onions are clear). Add tomato paste, tomatoes with chilies, sugar, Worcestershire sauce, chopped garlic, and the juice from two lemons along with the fish stock, and cook over a low fire 250-300°F for about 2 hours. Add flour and water as needed to maintain the desired courtbouillon (soup) consistency. For best results, this should be cooked over an open campfire outdoors.

About 20-30 minutes before serving add the seasoned fish strips, and 5 minutes before serving add the onion tops, and 2 sliced lemons. Sprinkle chopped parsley over dish before serving. Serve this dish over popcorn rice in gumbo bowls. Serve with fresh green salad and hot garlic French bread.

*6-8 servings*

# TROUT CYPREMORT

8 Speckled trout fillets
1 cup flour
1 tablespoon Creole or
Cajun seasoning

¼ stick butter
2 tablespoons olive oil

Heat olive oil and ¼ stick of butter on medium heat in frying pan. Season fillets with seasoning. Dredge fillets in flour. Fry 4 fillets until golden brown - remove and place on baking sheet in 250°F oven. Add ¼ stick of butter to pan and fry remaining 4 fillets the same way - place on baking sheet and cover with crab sauce. Heat in oven 20 minutes and serve hot.

**Crab Sauce:**
½ stick butter
1 large can sliced
mushrooms
1 package frozen mixed
seasonings

¼ cup white wine (sherry)
1 tablespoon lemon pepper
1 pound white lump
crabmeat
¼ can mushroom soup

Heat butter in frying pan. Sauté mixed seasonings until limp. Add lemon pepper, mushroom soup, mushrooms, wine and heat 15 minutes; stir occasionally. Add crabmeat and heat on medium heat for 15 minutes; stir occasionally without breaking up lump crabmeat.

## LAGNIAPPE SECTION

## BLACKENED FISH

Cajun chef Paul Prudhomme invented blackened fish, a dish in which caramelized butter and seasonings are applied to a fish fillet as it is seared in a hot, cast iron skillet. Fillets of redfish, pompano, red snapper, or salmon steaks are ideal for blackening. The resulting dish is superb! The cooking process, however, generates considerable smoke, and, wherever possible, you should cook blackened fish either outdoors or in a well-ventilated area. Blackened fish should be served piping hot on preheated plates and ramekins.

The ingredients below are sufficient to blacken six-to-eight, 8-ounce fillets cut ½-inch thick. (Do not use fillets thicker than ¾-inch.)

**1 teaspoon onion powder**          **1 teaspoon cayenne pepper**
**¾ teaspoon oregano**               **2 teaspoons salt**
**¾ teaspoon thyme**                 **4 teaspoons paprika**
**1 teaspoon black pepper**          **1 teaspoon garlic powder**
**1 teaspoon white pepper**

Mix seasonings then set aside. Heat a cast-iron skillet on a very high flame until the pot stops smoking and white ash forms on the bottom of the cooking surface. Warm serving plates in an oven set to 225°F. Melt ¾ pound of butter in a second skillet. Place 2 tablespoons of this melted butter in each ramekin and then set the dishes aside in a warm place. Coat each side of the fillets with melted butter. Sprinkle and then pat the seasoning mix onto each side of the fillets. Be sure that each fillet is thoroughly seasoned. Place the fillets in skillet, covering the upper sides with 1 tablespoon of melted butter. When the underside appears charred (about 2½ minutes are normally required), turn over the fillets and again pour 1 tablespoon of butter on the upper side of each fillet. When the underside is charred, remove the fillet from the skillet, put it in a ramekin, and serve it immediately on a hot serving plate.

# BATTER PREPARATION FOR FRYING

Cajuns born and raised in a fisherman's paradise have few equals in frying fish. The meal and batter recipes to follow have won acclaim among those who are hard to please.

## MEAL MIX #1

**(FOR FISH & FOWL)**

2 pounds self rising flour
1 pound white corn meal
1 pound yellow corn flour (fine)
11* tablespoons cayenne pepper
11 tablespoons garlic powder
5 tablespoons onion powder
4* tablespoons white pepper
*reduce pepper if want mild

## BATTER MIX #1

1 pint mustard
1 pint buttermilk
2 tablespoons universal Cajun mix*
1 tablespoon hot sauce
*or 1 tablespoon each cayenne, garlic powder, and black pepper

Mix meal and mix and batter separately. Store in refrigerator until ready to use.

## MEAL MIX #2

**(FOR SHRIMP, OYSTER & ALLIGATOR)**

2 pounds self rising flour
3 tablespoons cayenne pepper
3 tablespoons garlic powder
1 tablespoon onion powder
1 tablespoon white pepper

## BATTER MIX #2

12 egg whites
3 tablespoons vinegar
3 tablespoons baking powder

Mix meal and batter separately. To mix batter, whisk egg whites and add baking powder; when ready to fry add vinegar; when becomes foamy, dip shrimp and roll in meal mix twice; fry and drain on absorbent paper.

**Points to consider to help assure success in frying are:**

1. Pork lard at 300°F is preferred in home frying. Vegetable oil at 280°F is also good to fry.

2. In the absence of a thermometer, use white bread to determine if oil is hot enough. When the bread fries to a golden brown it is time to fry fish and/or potatoes.

3. An ideal method to dredge fish is to first dip it in the batter. Then shake it in a bag of meal mix until thoroughly covered with meal mix. Shake gently then fry.

4. Soaking French fry potatoes in batter and then dredging them in meal mix will add a new texture and flavor to the potatoes.

5. When fish are fried, drain on a cookie sheet which has been covered with a grease absorbing brown paper bag.

6. Do not salt fish or potatoes until after they are fried, as salt breaks down oil.

7. To prevent an oily burnt taste, filter oil before residues burn in the pot.

8. Meal mix can be made ahead of time and stored in cold storage to prevent seasoning break down.

9. Finally, it can be noted these meal and batter mixes are also ideal for frying crispy chicken, crawfish, shrimp, oysters, vegetables, etc.

# BOILED CRAWFISH, CRABS, AND SHRIMP

Crawfish boils have filled the void in Cajun society created by the passing of the *boucheries* (communal butcheries). Crawfish boils are—above all else—social gatherings, bringing together friends and relatives. Unlike most meals, crawfish boils generally last for hours, and participants use the gatherings to renew friendships and family ties, as well as an opportunity to catch up on news and gossip.

At crawfish boils, live crawfish are purged and then immersed in boiling water, along with ears of corn, onions, Irish potatoes, and plenty of crab boil seasoning. Preparing and cooking the crawfish is usually the exclusive domain of the men at the gathering—usually the host, assisted by one or two friends or relatives.

When fully cooked, the crawfish are removed from the cooking pots, drained, and then spread out on picnic tables for peeling. Peeled tails are dipped into sauces (usually a combination of catsup and mayonnaise) tailored to the tastes of individual participants.

The crawfish season is limited to the period from December to early June. The social gatherings continue after the crawfish season ends, but the focal point of the gathering becomes crabs and shrimp caught along the Louisiana Gulf Coast. The boiling techniques for crabs and shrimp are the same as those applied to crawfish.

### Equipment and Boiling Techniques

To boil 40 pounds of live crawfish, 2 dozen crabs, or 20 pounds of shrimp, use a 15-gallon pot with a cover, an internal, removable strainer, a gas burner, a butane or propane fuel tank, a large stirring spoon and gloves for use in seasoning the boiled shellfish, and a 48-quart ice chest. Use the ice chest to season and store the crawfish, shrimp, or crabs after they have been boiled. (Do not use a new ice chest for this purpose, for the heat of the boiled crawfish will warp the plastic container.) Once the boiled crawfish, shrimp, or crabs have been placed in the ice chest, elevate one side of the ice chest so that the juices rendered by the shellfish can drain out of the chest by means of the open drain plug. (You can also place a perforated tray one inch

above the juices to prevent over-seasoning of the shellfish by the fluids.)

### Serving Sizes

All recommended serving sizes should also include boiled corn on the cob or potatoes: 5 pounds of boiled crawfish, 1 pound of shrimp, or 6 medium crabs per person.

### Bob Richardson's Boiling Techniques

Bob Richardson, owner of Lafayette's Catfish Shak Restaurant and a local caterer, has prepared boiled crawfish, shrimp, and crabs for thousands of patrons. This is his recipe for boiled shellfish.

## CRAWFISH OR SHRIMP BOIL

**40 pounds of live crawfish, washed in clean, cool water**
**20 pounds of fresh shrimp with heads**
**2 dozen crabs**

**7 gallons of cold water**
**½ pound of salt**
**½ pint of liquid crawfish boil (optional)**
**1½ ounces of 80 degree cayenne pepper**

Place a 15-gallon pot on a gas burner; add seasonings; bring to a boil. Place 20 pounds of crawfish or shrimp in the 15-gallon pot by means of the insert strainer. Carefully lower the shellfish into the boiling water. Cover the pot. Check the water periodically. Once the water has begun to boil again, allow the shellfish to boil for 3 minutes. Turn off the fire and allow the shellfish to set in seasoned water for 3 additional minutes. Remove the shellfish from the pot by means of the internal strainer and then pour the contents into the ice chest. Pour some universal Cajun mixture over each layer to provide additional flavor. Keep the chest closed so that the shellfish will continue to steam and absorb seasonings.

Before boiling a second batch of shellfish, add ¼ pound of salt, ¼ pint of liquid crab boil, and ½ ounce of red pepper to the water. Then repeat the boiling and steaming process.

Crabs: Use the same boiling procedure as with crawfish and shrimp with this exception: Double the amount of red pepper in the water, but reduce the amount of dry seasoning mix by 50 percent when placing the crabs in the chest.

Vegetables: Potatoes, corn on the cob, whole onions, garlic pods, carrots and broccoli are commonly boiled in the same water as the seafood. Boil until tender, but taste the water for pepper and salt before placing vegetables in boiling water. If the water is too salty or too highly seasoned, dilute with additional water. When done, place the vegetables in a separate ice chest and sprinkle with universal seasoning mix.

## COLD BOILED SHRIMP

Chef Britt Shockley of *Broussard Catering* (Lafayette, La.) uses a unique technique to insure tasty, easy-to-peel shrimp.

**20 pounds fresh shrimp
   with heads
7 gallons water
1 gallon water for cold pack
   seasoning**

**4 gallons cubed ice
½ pound universal Cajun
   seasoning mix
2 large lemons, cubed
3 bay leaves**

Place a 15-gallon pot on the burner. Add 7 gallons of water, lemon, and bay leaves; bring the mixture to a boil; place the shrimp in a pot strainer; insert the strainer (with shrimp) into the boiling water. Keep the shrimp in the pot for one minute after the water again begins to boil. Remove the shrimp from the pot and let stand for one minute. Taste a sample. If necessary, return the shrimp to the boiling water for an additional minute. Be careful not to overcook, for overcooked shrimp will become tough and will cling to the shells. Place 1 gallon of water, ice, and seasonings in a 5-gallon vessel. Pour cooked shrimp from the insert strainer into the ice water. The cold water will cause the shells to open, thereby allowing the seasoning to come into contact with, and penetrate, the shrimp meat. Allow to stand in cold water for 10 minutes. During this time, adjust the seasonings to taste. Remove the shrimp and store them in a refrigerator until served.

# CAJUN SEASONINGS

Cajun cuisine has gained international notoriety over the last ten years. It now seems that anyone can cook some combination of highly peppered foods, call it "Cajun," and it sell it—at least once! Unfortunately, the secrets of traditional Cajun and Creole cuisines are not learned overnight, nor can they be gleaned from a cookbook—not even this one. One must have experienced the delicate nuances of flavor imparted by each of the many herbs and spices used in Cajun cooking and then have carefully committed to memory their individual effects on the main ingredients of recipes. The best cooks also know how mixtures of herbs, spices, and seasonings affect different meat or fish flavors.

Several commercial seasoning mixtures are currently available on your favorite supermarket shelves. The Tony Chachere, Paul Prudhommes, and Konriko labels are three of the more common brands. They are all what might be called basic Cajun seasoning mixes, which can be used in the preparation of any recipe, be it meat, fish, or fowl. You can make your own basic Cajun seasoning mix by combining the following ingredients:

**10 tablespoons salt**
**5 tablespoons red cayenne pepper**
**1¼ tablespoon black or white pepper**
**1½ tablespoon garlic powder**

**1½ tablespoon onion powder**
**1¾ tablespoon paprika**
**1¼ tablespoon MSG or accent (this is optional)**

This seasoning mixture should be stored in a relatively cool, dark area. It can be used without alteration for making gravies or sauces or as a rub-in seasoning for meat, fish, or fowl prior to cooking. It can also be added to marinating fluids such as vinegar, water, wine, pineapple juice, coca cola, or beer, depending on the taste you're striving to achieve. Add ¼ pound of seasoning to 30 ounces of water and blend for injecting into a 12-to-15-pound turkey. Use half the mixture for injecting and the other half for basting. The best method for injecting liquid seasoning into meat or fowl is to use a 2 ounce or 60 cc syringe with a removable "milk needle". A milk needle is blunt at the end and has one large orifice staggered or offset on each side of its shaft.

Before using the needle the first time file the blunt end to a sharp point.

As noted elsewhere, this is a basic all-purpose seasoning. Other herbs or spices can and should be added to it in order to enhance the flavor of a particular food. For example, if you were making sausage, you would add sage, or, if you were doing a lamb dish, you would add rosemary and garlic. In gumbo you would add filé, which is ground sassafras leaves. Any fish dish would require the addition of thyme. If the fish dish is bouillabaisse you would also add saffron.

Although onion, celery, and green bell pepper are not technically seasonings, they are so basic to Cajun and Creole cuisine that it is appropriate to include them in this section. Whether you make a roux prior to cooking gumbo, courtbouillon, sauce picante, or étouffée, you still need to sauté a mixture of finely chopped onions, celery, and bell pepper. Onions, celery, and bell pepper are sometimes called the holy trinity of Cajun cooking and are so widely used in Acadiana that they are available freshly chopped at our supermarket produce counters in one pint plastic containers.

Now that we have given you the "basics" why not head for the kitchen and begin to experience the pleasure and joy we Cajuns have long derived from the cooking experience.

# MY FIRST SOLO HUNT

Every young Cajun hunter dreams of spending the night at a duck camp without adult supervision. This first solo outing is a hunter's rite of passage. When I was fifteen years old, I made my first solo hunt at Ivy Richard's camp at Intracoastal City, Louisiana. Ivy's son Danny, Donald Frederick, and I hunted ducks in the afternoon. We cleaned the ducks killed, and then set off for the camp. Armed with onions, celery, bell peppers, and mothers' recipes, we prepared to cook the birds. The ducks still had some feathers when we ate them with our blood-red gravy and our five cups of rice cooked in a porcelain tea kettle, which produced enough rice for an army. I still hunt in that marsh, and, although that camp no longer exists, I shall never forget my memories of my first solo hunt.

# Cajun MEN COOK
## POULTRY
## & GAME

# POULTRY AND GAME

## "WIFE WENT TO BED SICK" CHICKEN DINNER

4 boneless, skinless chicken
  breasts, seasoned lightly
1 8 ounce can tomato sauce
½ cup water
¼ cup garlic sauce
1 bell pepper

1 small onion
grated Romano or Parmesan
  cheese
1 tablespoon of cooking oil
pasta (noodles or spaghetti)

Place chicken in oiled skillet, brown well. Add tomato sauce, water and garlic sauce over chicken. Cover and lower the heat to simmer and cook for 20 minutes. Place onion and bell pepper rings over chicken and sprinkle liberally with cheese (your choice). Re-cover and simmer for 10 minutes more. When done, serve over pasta.

*4 servings*

**Pork chops can be substituted.**

## FRENCH CHICKEN PASTA

1 fryer
2 bell peppers, chopped
1 large can mushrooms

1 can Parmesan cheese
1 package egg noodles
½ pound grated cheese

White Sauce:
3 tablespoons flour
2 tablespoons butter

2 cups milk

Boil fryer and take off skin and debone. Cut into small pieces. Save broth from fryer. In chicken fat, sauté the bell peppers until tender, set aside. Make a white sauce with flour, butter and milk. To white sauce that has been seasoned with salt and pepper and ½ can of Parmesan cheese, add mushrooms and diced chicken. Boil noodles in chicken broth until tender, drain and layer in a casserole dish with chicken mixture, then add cheese and bake at 350°F for 35 minutes. Can be increased very easily. Use larger chicken!

*8 servings*

**This is a very good recipe and is easy to make.**

## BASIC SAUCE PIQUANTE RECIPE

1 cup cooking oil
1 large (heaping) serving
   spoon of all purpose flour
2 onions, chopped fine
½ lemon, chopped fine
   (pulp and zest only)
1 bell pepper, chopped fine
2 stalks celery, chopped
   fine

1 medium can whole
   tomatoes
1 small can tomatoes with
   chilies, mashed
1 small can tomato paste
green onion tops, chopped
   fine
2 teaspoons Worcestershire
   sauce

Heat cooking oil and flour together until golden brown (makes roux). Add onions and cook for about 4 minutes. Add whole tomatoes, tomatoes with chiles, and tomato paste to roux. Stir and immediately add celery, bell peppers and lemons. Reduce heat to medium, let cook until oil rises to top, about one-half hour. Add water (amount depends on whether a thick or thin sauce is desired). Add salt and red pepper to taste. (Note: If using seafood it requires a lot of seasoning). Let mixture cook from 45 minutes to 1 hour, adding water or stock made from ingredients to be used as needed. Add any one of the following, and cook for another 15 to 20 minutes:

(a) shrimp and crabmeat
(b) chicken breasts which
   have been browned and
   cut into bite-size pieces
(c) rabbit which has been
   thoroughly browned

(d) any other type of
   ingredient which will go
   well with above basic
   sauce

Just before serving add 2 teaspoons of Worcestershire sauce plus green onion tops.

# GRANDMA CLAUDIA'S SMOTHERED CHICKEN

Men, let's be honest with ourselves. Our mamas, grandmas, sisters, 'ti-tantes (aunts), and nannans (godmothers) nurtured our innate culinary skills. As toddlers, we saw, smelled, and tasted the delicious results of their awesome cooking abilities. It should surprise no one that we learned much from them.

My culinary education was not exceptional. After serving in the Korean War, I enrolled in the agriculture program at Southwestern Louisiana Institute (present-day University of Southwestern Louisiana). Trying to support my three children, with my wife's able assistance, until I could receive my college degree, I cut corners wherever possible. I participated in a carpool with other students from Rayne, and I ate many noontime meals in my mother-in-law's kitchen.

My mother-in-law, Grandma Claudia Clement, was a Cajun-bred country girl who had mastered the art of transforming the typical Cajun noontime meal of rice, meat, and brown gravy into a feast. But, as Grandma Claudia was an avid soap-opera viewer, I always had to fend for myself in her kitchen at lunch time. (I still vividly recall her daily admonition: "Mais, you on you own! I have to watch As the Ball Roll [As the World Turns]." To feed myself, I used many of the culinary secrets that Grandma Claudia had passed on to me. She, in turn, had acquired these secrets from her Acadian ancestors—the LeBlancs, who had been expelled by the British from Nova Scotia in 1755.

125

## GRANDMA CLAUDIA'S SMOTHERED CHICKEN

1 2 pound fryer, cut in
pieces
½ cup cooking oil
1 cup chopped onion
½ cup chopped celery
½ cup cold water
1 teaspoon salt
¼ teaspoon pepper
¼ teaspoon garlic powder
⅛ teaspoon cayenne pepper
1 teaspoon corn starch
1 tablespoon brown sugar
2 tablespoons chopped
parsley
2 tablespoons chopped
onion tops

Wash and dry chicken parts; rub in oil, and season thoroughly. Heat the rest of the oil in a black iron pot. Fry all chicken parts to a golden brown. When done, remove the chicken and the oil and caramelize the sugar. Return the meat to the pot to glaze for about 5 minutes. Add vegetables with 2 tablespoons of oil and sauté on simmer; cover pot for about 5 minutes. Add ½ cup of warm water. Then simmer in covered pot for about 5 minutes. Add onion tops and parsley to hot gravy. Return chicken to pot and prepare to serve.

## CHICKEN À LA PROVENÇAL

6 tablespoons oil
4 pounds chicken parts,
rinsed and dried
2 cups green pepper strips
1½ pounds (4 medium)
tomatoes
2 cloves garlic, crushed
1 bay leaf
¼ teaspoon thyme
2 cups sliced onion
¼ pound spicy sausage
2 teaspoon salt
¼ teaspoon ground black
pepper
2 tablespoons flour
½ cup water

Heat oil in a 5 quart Dutch oven. Add chicken a few pieces at a time. Brown slowly on all sides over medium heat. Remove pieces as browned. Sauté green pepper strips in same oil about 5 minutes. Add tomatoes, garlic, bay leaf, and thyme and sauté 5 minutes. Return chicken pieces to Dutch oven. Add onion and sausage. Sprinkle with salt and pepper. Heat to boiling. Simmer covered for 30 minutes - until chicken is tender. To thicken sauce, stir flour into water, add to pot. Heat, stirring until sauce boils. Serve over rice. Great tasting dish!

*6 servings*

# CAJUN PAELLA

| | |
|---|---|
| 1 tablespoon seasoned salt | 2 tablespoons dried Italian |
| 1 can artichoke hearts | seasoning |
| 1 tablespoon turmeric | 2 cans broth |
| 3 cups converted rice | 2 tablespoons olive oil |
| 2 bell peppers, sliced thin | 2 pounds diced raw chicken |
| 2 pounds sliced smoked | 1 pound diced tasso |
| sausage | 2 pounds peeled shrimp |
| 2 1 pound cans diced | 2 large onions, diced |
| tomatoes | 1 can French onion soup |
| | 1 pound frozen green peas |

In a large non-stick pot, heat olive oil until smoking and brown diced chicken, sausage and then tasso. Add diced onions and continue until onions are wilted and beginning to brown. Reduce heat to medium high, add peeled shrimp, tomatoes, onion soup, Italian seasoning and salt. Mix well, let simmer 20 minutes. Add bell pepper, artichokes and any other vegetables desired (tomato, green beans) reduce heat to low. Cook three cups converted rice according to package directions substituting broth for water. Add 1 tablespoon turmeric to rice for color. Mix together meat and rice, garnish with parsley and green onions.

*12-15 servings (Can be cut in half to serve 6-8)*

# QUICK CHICKEN DIVAN

| | |
|---|---|
| 1 14 ounce package Swiss | 2 9 ounce packages frozen |
| fondue mix (prepared | broccoli |
| according to directions) | 18 slices cooked chicken or |
| | turkey |

Prepare Swiss fondue mix. Partially cook frozen broccoli until warm but not too tender. Butter a casserole dish. Preheat oven to 400°F. Layer chicken slices, broccoli and fondue, ending with fondue on top. Sprinkle with paprika or parsley. Bake about 10 minutes or until fondue is bubbling and slightly browned.

*6 servings*

**If you wish, you may layer coarsely crumbled crackers in the casserole as well.**

## CHICKEN MARENGO

| | |
|---|---|
| 1 small roasting chicken | 2 tablespoons butter |
| 1 cup dry white wine | 1 cup chicken bouillon |
| 3 tablespoons oil | 1 tablespoon chopped |
| 1-2 tablespoons tomato | shallots |
| paste | mushrooms |

Cut a small roasting chicken into serving pieces. Heat 3 tablespoons oil and 2 tablespoons butter. Sauté chicken in oil and butter until golden on all sides. Add 1 tablespoon chopped shallots, salt and pepper, 1 cup dry white wine and cook until wine is reduced to about half. Add 1 to 2 tablespoons tomato paste and 1 cup chicken bouillon. When chicken is tender, arrange pieces on heated platter. Reduce the sauce slightly. If the sauce needs thickening, stir in 1 tablespoon butter blended thoroughly with 1 tablespoon flour and cook for a few minutes longer. Put mushrooms on the chicken; strain the sauce over the chicken and serve hot.

## WHOLE ROAST CHICKEN

| | |
|---|---|
| 4 tender young chickens | ¼ teaspoon pepper |
| (about 2½ pounds each, | ½ teaspoon salt |
| clean and save the hearts, | 8 bay leaves |
| livers and gizzards) | ½ pound wild rice |
| 2 cups onions | 2 eggs, lightly beaten |
| butter | 12 strips of bacon |
| ½ teaspoon ground garlic | rosemary |
| ¼ pound chopped beef | salt and pepper to taste |
| ½ pound sausage | |

In a deep saucepan, sauté the onions in butter until brown. Add the ground garlic and let simmer. In a separate sauce pan, sauté the chicken livers, hearts, and gizzards with ¼ pound chopped beef and ½ pound sausage in olive oil. When brown, add to onions and garlic. At this time, also add pepper, salt, and bay leaves. Let simmer 10 minutes and add to the wild rice, which has cooked but not over-cooked and is still firm. Add eggs, lightly beaten, and blend. Stuff mixture into chickens. Place in roasting pan. Cover with abut 12 strips of bacon, sprinkle with rosemary, salt and pepper. Cook in 400°F oven about 45 minutes; baste frequently and turn after 25 minutes.

## POULET AU CHAMPIGNON

2 spring chickens
1 4 ounce can mushrooms
2 medium onions, chopped
1 jigger sherry wine
¼ pound butter
1 clove garlic

thyme
parsley
bay leaf
salt, red pepper and black
  pepper to taste

Cut chickens as for frying; season well with salt, black pepper and red pepper. Put chicken and butter in pot and brown slightly, add onion and cover tightly. Cook over low heat without adding water for about an hour. Add mashed garlic, thyme, bay leaf and parsley and cook for twenty minutes. Add sherry and mushrooms and cook another ten minutes and serve on hot toast.

## SMOTHERED GIZZARDS

1 pound gizzards
1 large onion, chopped
1 jalapeño pepper, chopped
2 links Andouille sausage
1 cup water

red pepper and salt to taste
3 tablespoons
  Worcestershire sauce
dash hot pepper sauce
1 tablespoon vegetable oil

Heat vegetable oil in a black iron pot. Meanwhile, season gizzards with salt and pepper. Brown gizzards in black iron pot on medium low heat. Stir in onions and peppers after gizzards have browned. Smother onions and peppers with gizzards then add 1 cup of water. Set fire to medium and cover pot. Cook for 10 minutes and then add 3 tablespoons of Worcestershire sauce and a dash of hot pepper. Cover and cook for another 15 minutes then add Andouille sausage, cover and set fire to medium low for 30 minutes. Serve over cooked rice.

*4 servings*

# FRIED TURKEY

| | |
|---|---|
| 2 10-12 pound turkeys | ⅓ cup chopped bell peppers |
| 1 large onion, minced | or jalapeño |
| 8-10 cloves garlic, peeled, | 2-3 tablespoons salt |
|   left whole | 2 tablespoons cayenne |
| |   pepper |

Clean turkeys thoroughly, leaving the skin flap at the neck intact. In a small mixing bowl, combine the minced onion, whole garlic, chopped peppers, 1½ tablespoons of salt and 1 tablespoon of cayenne pepper. With a sharp boning knife, make slits in the breasts and upper thighs of the turkeys and stuff the seasoning mix into the slits with your fingers. Pack well. Season the outside of the turkeys with the remaining salt and cayenne pepper. Place them in large plastic bags and refrigerate overnight. Before you begin frying, you do have to do a little preparation. First of all, do not try to fry them indoors. It can be dangerous as oil will splatter and may cause a fire; and, because of the smoke, your smoke detectors may be set off. You will need a butane burner and a large deep pot with a cover. Place cardboard and several layers of newspapers under the burner to protect your patio, deck or yard from grease splatters. Also, have on hand two large paper bags and two long-handled forks, like the kind you use for barbecuing. Pour enough cooking oil (may use peanut oil, but lard is the best) to fill the pot ¾ full. Oil must be at 350°F before adding the turkey. Holding the turkey by the neck skin flap, gently submerge the turkey into the hot oil. Be careful as the hot grease may overflow and splatter. Cover pot. Every 10 minutes, using the long-handled forks, turn the turkey around in the pot. It will take 45 minutes to 1 hour to cook one turkey. When the legs start to spread open, the turkey is done. Remove the turkey and put it inside the large paper bag and close tightly. Let it stand for 20 minutes before removing and carving.

# TURKEY WITH BREAD DRESSING

**Dressing:**

2 loaves white bread (24 ounces each)

4-5 medium onions, chopped

6 ribs celery, chopped

4 teaspoons poultry seasoning

salt and pepper to taste

Toast white bread and tear in small pieces. Sauté onions and celery until soft. Add enough water to the bread to moisten thoroughly, but not sloppy. Add onions and celery and poultry seasoning. Add salt and pepper to taste. This makes enough dressing for a 20-24 pound turkey with some left over which can be baked in a separate bowl.

**Turkey:**

1 20 pound turkey

margarine or butter

flour

water

salt and pepper to taste

Pat dry the turkey cavities and rub in salt and pepper. Stuff the turkey cavities and sew together. Salt and pepper the outside of turkey and place in baking pan. Cover the turkey with a white cloth basted with margarine or butter, place lid on pan and bake at 350°F until done, about 5 hours. Make gravy using the drippings by mixing flour and water then stirring into the drippings over medium heat. When thickened, stir in water to desired consistency.

*25 to 30 servings*

***Toast the bread and cook the onions and celery before but do not mix together until ready to stuff the turkey.***

## BIG TURKEY'S ITALIAN GOBBLER SPAGHETTI SAUCE

2 pounds "Italian" turkey sausage
2 pounds ground turkey meat
3 large onions, chopped
1 large bell pepper, chopped
1 head celery, chopped
2 pounds fresh mushrooms, sliced thin
4 cloves garlic, chopped fine
2 large jars spicy Italian spaghetti sauce

In a large Magnalite roaster, brown turkey sausage well (medium fire); remove and slice thin. Sauté onions, bell pepper, celery and garlic (10 minutes); add ground turkey; brown with sautéed onions, etc. (Hint: This keeps ground turkey from lumping together) After ground turkey is browned well add sliced sausage, spaghetti sauce and sliced mushrooms. Add salt and pepper to taste. Lower fire and simmer for 90 minutes stirring occasionally. Serve over pasta.

*6-8 servings*

# THE HUNTING CAMP

Our deer hunting group gathered at the cabin two days before the season opened each year. We would clean the cabin, put in a store of firewood, stow our gear and provisions, and draw straws to determine who did the cooking each day. Anyone who brought liquor was required to place it on an open shelf opposite the fireplace where it could be seen by everyone. The shelf generally held everything from the cheapest whiskey to Crown Royal and Chevis Regal. We all felt strongly that booze and guns don't mix.

I had made a huge pot of gumbo that fed everyone the second night. Hebert was to do the cooking on opening day, and he was not overjoyed at the prospect of missing the first day's hunt.

The night before the season opened we played poker, had a few drinks and enjoyed the camaraderie that prevails at all hunting camps. Hebert, who was never shy about drinking, consumed more than his share that night, probably out of frustration about missing the next day's hunt.

The fire had burned itself out during the night and the cabin was very cold at dawn. Three of the group were awake and each was waiting for the other to get up and rekindle the fire. At about that time, Hebert who was badly hung over, bolted from his bunk, ran out the door and vomited. He came back in, went to the shelf and took a swig of Crown Royal and again ran out and upchucked. By now, everyone was awake and Thibodeaux was getting the fire going. When Hebert came in and approached the shelf again, a voice from the far corner of the still dimly lighted cabin was heard to say, "Hebert, why don't you use the cheap stuff as long as you're just practicing?"

## GOURMET VENISON ROAST

**Roast:**

1 5 pound venison roast
2 cups water
1 cup white vinegar
2 tablespoons vegetable oil
½ cup dry red wine
1 teaspoon meat tenderizer
2 tablespoons salt
1 tablespoon black pepper
¼ teaspoon cayenne red pepper
½ teaspoon garlic powder
3 garlic cloves, chopped fine

1 large onion, chopped fine
1 medium bell pepper, chopped fine
2 stalks celery with leaves, chopped fine
3 sprigs parsley, chopped fine
4 sprigs onion tops, chopped fine
2 lemons, sliced in rounds
8 slices bacon

Prepare roast by removing outer membrane skin, and marinate in refrigerator overnight in ice water and vinegar. Remove roast and dry well with towel. Set aside. Sauté vegetables except onion tops and parsley in roasting pan in oil until limp, about 5 minutes. Place roast in a roasting pan. Brush wine over roast, and season with meat tenderizer, salt, black and red pepper, and garlic powder. Place lemon slices on top of roast; place bacon on top of lemon slices and hold down with toothpicks.

**Sauce:**

½ cup butter
½ cup honey
½ cup fresh orange juice

½ teaspoon rosemary
3 tablespoons dry red wine
8 quart roaster

Melt butter in double boiler; add honey, orange juice, rosemary, and wine. Baste roast well with sauce and place covered in 275°F oven. Cook for 4 hours, basting frequently with sauce. Remove cover and cook 1 more hour. Remove roast from pot. Dissolve cornstarch in 2 tablespoons of warm water. Stir and simmer to desired thickness. Add warm water to thin, if needed. Add parsley and onion tops, return roast, cover with gravy and simmer 3 minutes. Remove roast, carve and serve over rice and gravy.

*8 servings*

## BARBECUE VENISON ROAST

1 venison roast
(approximately 5-7
  pounds)
½ gallon buttermilk
1 box garlic (2 cloves)

24 small red hot peppers
1 onion
salt, red pepper and black
  pepper

Light barbecue pit and place coals as far away from the meat as possible. Let coals get white. Season roast well with salt, red pepper and black pepper. Stuff the roast with garlic pods and red hot peppers. Chop up the onion and put the seasoned roast in a pan with the onion and buttermilk for one or two days to marinate. The buttermilk draws the wild taste but does not give a vinegary taste. Put the roast on a rotisserie and let your pit cool down to approximately 400°F. Let the roast cook about 2½ to 3 hours. The rotisserie keeps the roast moist and it will not dry out.

*6-8 servings*

## LIL' PRAIRIE HUNTING CLUB DEER ROAST

1 deer ham roast, deboned
1 bottle hot barbecue sauce
15-20 strips bacon
3 bell peppers, chopped fine

3 large onions, chopped fine
8 cloves garlic, chopped
  fine
seasoning to taste

Debone a deer ham roast - slice large slits in roast - fill each slit with a strip of bacon - fill slits with garlic, onion and bell pepper. Sprinkle seasoning over roast. Roll roast and tie with cotton twine. Brown on barbecue fire on high heat. Remove roast and wrap in heavy duty tin foil so it is waterproof; before closing foil, pour one bottle of hot barbecue sauce over roast. Cook on low fire on side of barbecue pit (do not place directly over hot coals). Cook 3½ hours - do not puncture foil. Remove, slice and enjoy.

## LIL' PRAIRIE FRIDAY STEW

Lil' Prairie is twenty minutes South of Kaplan on Louisiana Hwy. 35. On the way to Lil' Prairie Hunting Club on Friday evening, we always bring a can of orange spray paint. On the way down, we spray all the roadkills we see on the road with orange paint. Then we go to the Lil' Prairie Lounge and enjoy a cool six pack. After an hour or two, we send a designated driver to Kaplan to gather all the roadkills without orange spray paint. In this way, we're assured of fresh meat for supper, using the following procedure: Clean game—drink more beer. Cook stew—drink more beer. Enjoy—with beer.

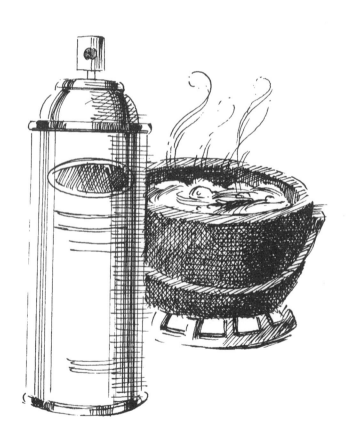

## VENISON MEAT LOAF

2 pounds venison, ground
1 pound pork sausage, loose
1 pound ground beef
2 eggs, fresh
4 eggs, boiled
1 cup onions, finely
 chopped
½ cup celery, finely
 chopped
½ cup bell pepper, finely
 chopped

4 garlic cloves, minced
½ cup onion tops, chopped
½ cup parsley, chopped
1 cup bread crumbs, plain
2 teaspoons dry mustard
1 teaspoon salt
½ teaspoon red pepper
½ teaspoon black pepper
¼ teaspoon thyme
½ teaspoon basil
1 cup milk

Mix meats. Mix dry seasonings together. Then add to meat, slightly beaten eggs and rest of ingredients. Use milk as needed to moisten meat mix. Form a meat loaf and fit in bread pan. Arrange boiled eggs cut in half on the sides and top of loaf. Bake approximately 2 hours at 350°F. Serve with buttered grits, lima beans, hot biscuits, and Mayhaw or Muscadine jelly. Cha-a! (Key-Yah), that's good, Yea.

*6 servings*

## FRANCKA BEEF JERKY

2 pounds deer meat, sliced
 ⅛-¼ inch thick (put in
 freezer 1 hour for easier
 slicing)
¼ cup soy sauce

1 tablespoon Worcestershire
 sauce
½ teaspoon onion salt
¼ cup liquid smoke
¼ teaspoon black pepper
¼ teaspoon garlic salt

Mix all ingredients and pour over meat; work into meat thoroughly; marinate over night. Place foil over oven racks; lay meat on foil. Bake at 200°F for 4 hours or until it bends but does not break. Wedge a knife in door facing to allow moisture to escape. Let cool and either place in airtight jars or freeze.

**A modern dehydrator can be used instead of the oven.**

# CROCK POT GAME

1 deer or elk roast (or beef roast with fat removed)
2 tablespoons olive oil
5-6 large carrots
5-6 whole red potatoes
1 large onion
1 large bell pepper
3-5 green onions
4-5 toes garlic
1 package fresh mushrooms
1 cup red wine
2 beef bouillon cubes
*seasoned dried parsley, oregano, garlic powder, salt, pepper, mint and ½ tablespoon Worcestershire sauce

Start with roast 3 to 5 pounds, cut into 5 to 6 large chunks. Season chunks well with season salt and pepper. Char well on gas grill on high or in a skillet. Sear with butter. Set aside. Coat a crock pot with 1 tablespoon olive oil. Add carrots in chunks, potatoes in chunks, onion chopped bell pepper chopped, green onions chopped, garlic and mushrooms whole. Add season and spice: parsley, oregano, garlic powder, salt, pepper and mint. Add set aside meat, 1 cup of red wine, 1½ cups of water, 2 beef bouillon cubes, ½ tablespoon Worcestershire sauce. You can use flour or corn starch to thicken to your taste. Cover crock pot and cook all day on high. Serve with French bread and butter.

## BUBBA'S GAME KABOBS

2 pounds cubed deer,
    antelope or elk meat from
    roast
bacon slices
12 small white onions

2 bell peppers, cut up in
    about 2 inch squares
1 pound small cherry
    tomatoes

Marinade:
1 bottle Italian salad
    dressing
2 cups white wine

1 tablespoon garlic powder
½ teaspoon hot sauce
salt and pepper

Combine marinade ingredients and meat cubes in covered dish overnight or at least for four hours. Reserve marinade. Wrap meat cubes in bacon and place on metal skewers alternating with cherry tomatoes, onions and bell peppers (mushrooms can also be used). Salt and pepper to taste and place on grill over hot charcoal or hardwoods. Turn kabobs frequently and baste with marinade until well done. Serve over brown/wild rice combination.

*4-5 servings*

## LA SAUCE DE CHASSEUR

5 pounds rabbit, duck,
    squirrel, chicken, etc.
½ cup onions, chopped fine
½ cup tart apple cider or
    white wine
2 16 ounce cans or two
    pounds of fresh ripe
    tomatoes
½ cup olive oil

1 bay leaf, crushed
¼ teaspoon basil
¼ teaspoon oregano
¼ teaspoon marjoram
1 4 ounce can mushroom
    stems and pieces
2 teaspoons salt
1 teaspoon black pepper

Cut meat into serving pieces and salt and pepper. Place in an 8 quart iron pot and brown in olive oil. Add onions and sauté until opaque. Add tomatoes and cider or wine. Sprinkle herbs all over. Cover and simmer 1½ hours. Partially open cover and simmer until sauce is at desired consistency. Adjust salt and pepper seasoning. Serve over rice.

*10 servings*

**Serve with toasted garlic French bread, a green salad and German wine.**

# RABBIT BOURGUIGNONNE

3 large rabbits, deboned
½ stick butter and 2
  tablespoons oil
¼ cup cognac
6 slices thick bacon
2 large onions, sliced long
¼ cup flour
8 ounces fresh mushrooms
2 cups burgundy wine

1 can beef consommé + 1
  cup of water
1 tablespoon tomato paste
2 cloves garlic, mashed
Bouquet Garni - thyme (1
  teaspoon)*
  parsley (handful)*
  bay leaves - 2*
* Tied in cheesecloth
salt and pepper to taste

Cut rabbit into 1 inch cubes - dry meat, use high heat and heavy pot - melt butter and oil and use as needed to brown meat (small amount at a time). To last batch of meat, when browned, add cognac (will flame) to collect sediment. Put all meat in pot; put remaining butter and oil in pot on high heat. Add bacon and onions and sauté until onions are soft, add ¼ cup of flour to meat, add mushrooms, wine, stock, tomato paste, garlic, bouquet garni and season. Cover and cook in 325°F oven for 2 hours - or - on top of stove, cook on low heat for 3 hours. Serve over rice or pasta - Enjoy!

# ACE DUCK CAMP HUNT

Hammy Patin has operated a commercial duck and geese hunting camp for many years. His lodge—located eight miles south of Kaplan, Louisiana—serves as headquarters for his 6,500-acre marsh and wetlands operation. The camp is in the heart of migratory duck and geese country. Hammy says, "The three main reasons why high profile clients keep coming back to hunt are good food, Cajun hospitality, and an assurance of game."

All of the ingredients necessary for the camp's success are present in a typical hunt. Clients typically arrive at the camp around 3:00 p.m. They are greeted by Hammy and his staff who serve refreshments and hors d'oeuvres. The renowned "Patin's Crawfish Dip" conditions the appetite for the camp special "Ace Camp Blue Goose and Hen Gumbo," started with a medium brown, homemade roux, diluted with water, and cooked with seasoned fowl, onions, garlic, bell peppers, and celery on simmer heat for three hours. Hammy says he knows of a Cajun who attempts to imitate his style by putting wine in his gumbo, but no real Cajun drinks wine while cooking and eating his gumbo!

Weekend guests are served crawfish étouffée during the second evening. Hammy advises, "Do not cook crawfish, shrimp, or oysters more than eight minutes if you want them to be juicy." Of course camaraderie, highlighted by a friendly laid-back atmosphere enlivened by Cajun humor, is the norm before bedtime. At 4:00 a.m., the clients are awaken by the aroma of Cajun coffee, milk, juices, fresh donuts, and rolls. After breakfast, the hunters are transported by boat to their duck or goose blinds just prior to day break. Hunters are assured of game through the presence of wild birds and locally raised mallard ducks. This local mallard program allows the season to stay open from October to April. By 10:00 a.m. a Cajun camp brunch awaits the returning hungry hunters. Men, women, and young adults are treated to such dishes as corn and crawfish maque choux, seasoned smothered pork roast stuffed with onions, garlic, and bell peppers, meatball stew, grillades (marinated thinly sliced pork smothered in onions and brown gravy), and crawfish omelets. All of this good stuff is topped with homemade biscuits, fig and pear preserves, pecan pies, bread pudding, and vanilla custard.

# OVEN ROASTED DUCK

| | |
|---|---|
| 4 large ducks | 1 can mushrooms |
| onions | green onions, chopped |
| apples | flour |
| red wine | salt and pepper to taste |
| orange juice | 1-2 bacon strips per duck |

Season ducks with salt and pepper, inside and out. Stuff with apple and onion. Put in roasting pan and sprinkle flour on the ducks. Place 1 or 2 strips of bacon. Add red wine and orange juice (1 cup of wine to ½ cup of juice). Cook uncovered in oven at 425°F for 20 minutes. Reduce heat to 325°F and add chopped green onion tops and mushrooms. Cover and cook 2 hours or until tender.

# DUCK-POT-ROASTED

| | |
|---|---|
| 2 wild ducks split in half, lengthwise | 2 teaspoons equal season mix of thyme, sage, marjoram, or rosemary |
| 1 large onion, quartered | |
| 4 carrots, sliced crosswise | 1 teaspoon salt |
| 2 ribs celery, quartered | ½ teaspoon black pepper |
| 6 new potatoes | ¼ teaspoon cayenne red pepper |
| 2 strips bacon | |
| 1 cup water | 6 quart cast iron pot |
| 1 cup red dry wine | |

Season halves generously with salt, pepper, and season mix. Place ducks in iron pot, pour wine and water over ducks and place ½ piece bacon strips on top of birds. Cover pot and bake in oven at 375°F for 1½ hours. Baste every 30 minutes. Add potatoes, cover pot and cook uncovered for an additional 1 hour. Baste as needed.

*4 servings*

# ELLENDERS' ROAST DUCK

1 duck

**Stuffing:**

1 clove garlic, sliced thin
2 celery stalks, quartered
½ medium apple, quartered
1 small onion, quartered
2 tablespoons bacon grease
salt and black pepper to
   taste
1 medium onion, chopped
   fine
1 bay leaf

1 clove garlic, chopped fine
¼ bell pepper, chopped fine
⅛ teaspoon thyme
⅛ teaspoon hot sauce
⅛ teaspoon Worcestershire
   sauce
¼ teaspoon salt
1 4 ounce can button
   mushrooms
3 tablespoons water

Inside and out, grease duck with bacon fat and salt and pepper to taste, about ¾ teaspoon salt and ½ teaspoon of black pepper (more if you like). Stab breast in a few places and insert slivers of garlic, Stuff cavity with apple and onion pieces. In a 6 quart iron Dutch oven, add onion, garlic, bell pepper, bay leaf, hot sauce, Worcestershire sauce, celery seasonings, and water. Add more water as needed as duck cooks to keep vegetables from burning. Place duck on rack in Dutch oven, cover, and bake in oven for about 1 hour at 350°F until duck is tender. Remove cover and brown duck on top of stove, about 10 minutes on medium low heat. Baste as needed. Remove duck, rack and pulp from pot, and make gravy. If desire thicker, dissolve 1 tablespoon of cornstarch in ½ cup of warm water and stir into drippings. Add mushrooms, adjust seasoning in gravy if needed. Add duck, and pulp, baste with gravy, cover and simmer, 5 minutes. Serve on rice with gravy.

*3 servings*

*This is one of the late Louisiana Senator Allen Ellender's recipes. He was acclaimed as a "Chef Supreme" by President Nixon as he served as President Pro Tem of the Senate.*

*Keep lid on tight so steam will permeate duck with seasonings.*

## CAJUN FRIED DUCK BREAST

2 duck breasts, each sliced
  in 3 pieces
1½ cup milk
1 teaspoon salt
½ teaspoon black pepper
⅛ teaspoon cayenne red
  pepper

2 eggs, beaten
1 cup saltine cracker
  crumbs
shortening, lard preferred
6 quart iron pot

Tenderize breasts slightly with meat hammer. Cut each breast into 3 equal pieces. Soak in milk for 2 hours. Remove duck from milk, dip in beaten eggs, sprinkle with salt and pepper, and dredge in finely crumbled cracker crumbs. Deep fry in large skillet with 1 inch of shortening at medium heat for 20 minutes on each side.

*4 servings*

## CREOLE DUCK

**Duck:**
2 wild ducks, cut into
  pieces
3 tablespoons butter
3 tablespoons olive oil

1 clove garlic, minced
½ pound fresh mushrooms,
  sliced
¾ cup beef stock

Salt and pepper pieces of duck and marinate overnight in refrigerator (see recipe below). In a heavy skillet, melt butter over medium heat; add olive oil and mix well. Cook until hot, then brown the pieces of duck until well browned on all sides, about 20 minutes. Add garlic, mushrooms and beef stock.

**Marinade:**
¾ teaspoon salt
½ teaspoon black pepper
¼ cup brandy
1 cup red wine
2 onions, chopped

1 tablespoon parsley,
  chopped
½ teaspoon marjoram
½ teaspoon allspice
6 quart roaster

Strain ½ cup of marinade and add to skillet. Cook until liquid begins to simmer, cover, reduce heat to low and cook covered, for 1½ hours.

*4 servings*

## BAR-B-QUE DUCK BREAST

Duck Breast
Italian salad dressing
onion

bell pepper
1 bacon strip per duck
breast

Cut breast meat off of breast bone. Marinate in Italian salad dressing at least 4 hours. Wrap each duck breast around a slice of onion and bell pepper (can also use a piece of jalapeño) in a strip of bacon. Hold together with toothpick. Cook on barbecue pit for approximately 40 minutes.

## BEE'S DRUNKEN WILD DUCK

2 wild ducks cut up like
  fryer
1 stick butter
salt and red pepper to taste
garlic powder

½ gallon burgundy wine
1 large can stems and
  pieces mushrooms
corn starch and water

Season the duck with salt, red pepper and garlic powder. Fry the pieces in the melted butter, removing the pieces until all has been browned. Put all of the pieces of duck back in the butter, cover with the wine, cook until tender, add mushrooms, and thicken with corn starch and water. Serve over rice.

145

# WILD RICE DUCK

2 wild ducks
1¼ teaspoon salt
¼ teaspoon red pepper
½ cup white wine
½ cup water
1 16 ounce package wild
  rice mixed with white rice
1 large onion, chopped

1 tablespoon bacon grease
1 rib celery, chopped
½ cup parsley, chopped
½ cup green onion tops
½ pound hot smoked
  sausage, crumbled fine
2 cloves garlic, minced

Cook duck in wine and water in covered cast iron pot at 350°F for 1½ hours. Remove and cut duck in pieces. Reserve juices. Cook rice according to directions in sauté pan. Sauté onion in cast iron pot with bacon grease until opaque color. Add celery, garlic, salt and pepper. Add rice to pot. Brown sausage in a small skillet, add a little water to clean drippings and place in iron pot. Add ducks to rice mixture, and ½ cup of reserved juices. Place in iron pot. Add seasonings and cook on stove, on low heat, covered, for 2 hours. Add parsley and onion tops, mix and then remove from heat. Serve hot.

*6 servings*

# DUCK À L'ORANGE

4½ to 5 pound duckling
⅔ cup orange marmalade
⅓ cup barbecue sauce

Seasoning to taste
Fruit of your choice

Sprinkle duckling with salt (and pepper, if desired). Place breast side up in shallow roasting pan. Cover loosely with aluminum foil. Bake in a preheated 425°F oven for 45 minutes. Prick skin occasionally. Reduce temperature to 325°F. Bake an additional 1½ hours. Pour off drippings. Remove foil cover. Continue roasting 45 minutes to 1 hour or until tender, brushing frequently with marmalade combined with barbecue sauce. Serve over rice, garnished with fruit, if desired.

Delicious!

*4-5 servings*

# SMOKING FOWL

When smoking turkeys, geese, or mature chickens, begin by defrosting the bird. Once the bird is defrosted remove all organs and then clean the bird thoroughly before patting it dry.

Mix one tablespoon of basic Cajun seasoning mix in two ounces of water per each pound of fowl meat. For example: a fifteen-pound bird requires fifteen tablespoons of Cajun seasoning mixed in thirty ounces of water.

Using a hypodermic syringe, inject all of the liquid seasoning into the breast, wings, legs, and thighs. Place the injected bird into a deep pot or crock and cover with marinade of the same seasoning liquid for up to seventy-two hours.

Remove bird from marinade, pat dry, and hang in a smoke chamber for one hour before starting fire. Place meat thermometer in the thickest part of the bird and start the fire. When the bird is fully smoked remove from chamber and allow to cool at least one hour before slicing.

Use the same procedure and ratios of seasoning for fryers and ducks but inject only one ounce of seasoning per pound of bird. Marinate as with turkey. See instructions and diagram on how to build a smoke house on pages 188 and 189, respectively.

# ROASTED GOOSE AND CITRUS STUFFING

**Roasted Goose:**

1 goose dressed, wild
  preferred
2 tablespoons bacon grease
  or oil
1 teaspoon salt

¼ teaspoon black pepper
⅛ teaspoon cayenne red
  pepper
¼ teaspoon garlic powder

Wash goods and dry thoroughly. Mix salt, pepper, and garlic powder together. Rub bacon grease inside and out of bird and season the same way. Place bird on a rack in a shallow pan and bake with breast up, uncovered for 1 hour at 350°F.

**Citrus Stuffing:**

4 cups plain croutons
2 cups cooked wild rice
3 tablespoons grated orange
  rind
1 teaspoon grated lemon
  rind
1 cup diced orange with
  white pulpy membrane
  removed
2 cups celery, diced
1 4 ounce can mushroom
  stems and pieces

½ tablespoon marjoram
½ tablespoon thyme
½ tablespoon rosemary
½ tablespoon poultry
  seasoning
¾ teaspoon salt
¼ teaspoon black pepper
½ cup melted butter
2 eggs, beaten
8 quart roaster

Combine the croutons, wild rice, orange and lemon rind, orange, celery and mushrooms. Add seasonings. Moisten the mixture with melted butter, beaten eggs and warm water. Stuff the bird, place in a roaster placing excess stuffing at the bottom of the pot around the goose. Bake covered for 1½ hours at 350°F. Last 20 minutes increase temperature to 375°F, and take cover off to brown bird.

*4 servings*

# GEESE AND DUCK RECIPE

Wash and dry geese/duck(s); do NOT remove fat.

**1 cup duck stock from drippings**
**2 cups clover honey**
**½ teaspoon lemon zest**

**1 cup Amaretto liqueur**
**2 tablespoons unsalted butter**

**Seasonings:**
**1 tablespoon salt**
**2 teaspoons paprika**
**1 teaspoon garlic powder**
**¾ teaspoon onion powder**

**¾ teaspoon white pepper**
**½ teaspoon black pepper**
**½ teaspoon thyme leaves**
**1 teaspoon red pepper**

Mix seasonings well and rub into bird. Liberally sprinkle birds with seasonings and rub down, wrap drumstick with foil. Set oven at 450°F. Place in large baking pan, **don't touch**; cook uncovered on middle rack for 30 minutes. Turn over, breast side down, bake 20 minutes more. Turn right side up and bake 10 minutes more. Remove and let cool - room temperature or fridge.

Amaretto Glaze: In a saucepan bring stock to gentle boil (drippings from pan). Stir honey, lemon zest and liqueur; cook over medium heat until sauce thickens - 20 minutes. Drop in butter and stir in sauce until shiny. Remove pan from heat and allow to blend. Preheat oven at 400°F, put cold duck/geese in pan for 25-30 minutes. Liberally brush with glaze, place back in oven until glaze sets. Repeat glazing until done - crust forms - 10 minutes. Enjoy!!!

# WILD GOOSE À LA CRÈME

1 goose, about 6 pounds
½ teaspoon garlic powder
¼ teaspoon paprika
1½ stalks celery, chopped
2 medium carrots, chopped
1 large onion, chopped
2 tablespoons bacon grease, preferred

4 tablespoons flour
½ teaspoon rosemary
¼ teaspoon thyme
1¼ teaspoon salt
1 cup thick sour cream
1 4 ounce can mushroom stems and pieces

Wash and dry goose, inside and outside. Remove neck and wing tips. Season inside and out with garlic powder, salt and paprika. Place on rack in shallow pan. Bake, uncovered, for one hour at 325°F until brown and fat has melted off. Discard drippings. Simmer in a sauce pan, giblets, neck and wing tips barely covered with water. Brown chopped celery, carrots, and onion in fat until soft and golden. Stir in 2 tablespoons of flour, then blend in liquid from giblets (1 cup stock). Season with rosemary, thyme and remaining salt. Stir remaining flour into sour cream to keep it from curdling during roasting. Blend into gravy. Remove goose from shallow pan and place in a roasting pan. Pour gravy and drained mushrooms over it. Cover and continue roasting another 2 hours or until tender.

*4 servings*

# GERMAN COVE ROAST GOOSE

2 cups sauerkraut
1 goose, wild preferred
1 apple, quartered
2 tablespoons butter
½ teaspoon dry mustard
2½ ounces Worcestershire
sauce

½ lemon, use juice
¼ cup red wine
¼ teaspoon paprika
1 cup boiling water

Salt and pepper goose inside and out and loosely stuff with sauerkraut and apple; secure cavity with toothpicks. Place goose on rack in a roasting pan and pour the boiling water at bottom of pan. Bake in oven at 325°F for 3 hours. About 30 minutes before the goose has cooked, make the sauce. Melt butter and simmer for 1 minute (DO NOT BROWN). Add Worcestershire sauce, mustard and paprika. Simmer for 20 minutes, then add wine and cook for 2 minutes on low fire. Add lemon juice just before serving. Remove goose from oven. Allow to cook for 10 minutes. Discard stuffing and carve. Pour sauce over individual servings.

*4 servings*

As a side treat boil new potatoes and carrots in salt water for 10 minutes. Then about 30 minutes before the goose is cooked place the potatoes and carrots in the pan alongside the bird. Use 1 tablespoon of salt for every quart of water used to boil vegetables.

## SIX STUFFED QUAIL

6 quail
¼ pound bacon
2 tablespoons parsley, chopped fine
5 shallots, chopped fine
6 slices white bread, oven dried and crumbled
1 stick of butter
2 teaspoons poultry seasoning
1 4 ounce can of mushroom stems and pieces with juice

¾ teaspoon salt
½ teaspoon black pepper
½ cup flour
1 stick butter
½ cup dry white wine
1 teaspoon fresh lemon juice
1 tablespoon Worcestershire sauce
1 teaspoon hot pepper sauce

Prepare stuffing: cut bacon in small pieces and fry until almost crisp; remove most of the grease and add shallots. Cook for 3 minutes. Add butter, parsley, poultry seasoning, bread crumbs, mushrooms with juice. If needed, add hot water to moisten. Salt and pepper quail inside and out. Fill cavities loosely with stuffing and dredge lightly in flour. Brown quail uniformly in butter in skillet and transfer to baking pan. Make gravy in skillet drippings by adding wine, lemon juice, Worcestershire sauce and pepper sauce. Pour gravy over quail, cover and roast for 45 minutes at 350°F. Baste a few times during the baking process.

**Another easy to make stuffing is to use ½ pound of Cajun boudin sausage. Remove from the casing and mix with ¼ teaspoon of sage.**

*3 servings*

# LA CRÈME QUAIL

6 quail, split in half
1 stick butter
½ onion, chopped fine
1 clove garlic, minced
¾ cup celery, chopped fine
½ cup boiling water
⅛ teaspoon thyme

⅛ teaspoon rosemary
⅛ teaspoon cayenne red
   pepper
1 teaspoon salt
1 cup dry wine
1 cup heavy cream
6 quart iron pot

Add quail to cast iron pot with melted butter, cook over low heat 5 minutes on each side. Add onion, garlic, bell pepper and celery and cook until birds are brown. Add boiling water, cover, and simmer for 30 minutes. Add salt, pepper, thyme, rosemary and wine, uncover and simmer for an additional 10 minutes. Remove quail to hot platter. Strain sauce, return to pot, add cream and heat until hot, about 10 minutes on low fire. Serve sauce separately over rice.

*4 servings*

# LEMON BUTTER QUAIL

8 quail
8 slices bacon
4 tablespoons fresh lemon
   juice, mince peelings of ½
   lemon
1 stick butter

¼ teaspoon red pepper
¼ teaspoon garlic powder
½ tablespoon parsley,
   minced
salt and black pepper to
   taste

Melt butter in skillet and add lemon juice, peelings and seasonings. Stir for 1 minute on low fire. Wrap bacon strip around each bird's breast and hold in place with tooth pick. Thoroughly baste each bird with sauce. Place breast down in 9x12 inch baking dish and drape with foil. Bake at 350°F for 1 hour. Baste occasionally to prevent drying out. After 45 minutes, remove foil, turn birds breast up and brown for 15 minutes. Remove birds if gravy is desired from drippings. Dissolve 1 teaspoon corn starch in two tablespoons of warm water and add to baking dish. Stir. Adjust seasonings. Put birds back in dish and baste with gravy before serving. Garnish with parsley.

*4 servings*

## SAUCED QUAIL

12 quail
1½ sticks butter
2 cups diced carrots
½ cup onions, chopped
  finely
½ cup bell pepper, finely
  chopped

12 ounces fresh
  mushrooms, sliced
2 tablespoons flour
1 cup chicken stock or
  broth from a can
2 cups dry white wine

Melt ½ butter and fry quail to a golden brown. Remove and set aside. Be careful not to puncture skin. Grease a 4 quart covered casserole and set aside. In original skillet add rest of butter and sauté all ingredients, except wine, 15 minutes on simmer. Remove mushrooms and set aside. Push vegetables through a strainer into sauce in skillet. Slowly add flour and chicken stock. Simmer for 5 minutes. In 350°F oven place quail, breast up, in covered casserole, baste with wine and bake for 15 minutes. Turn breast down, add sauce and bake for 45 minutes.

*6 servings*

# COCHON DE LAIT

According to Nicki Bordelon, *cochon de lait* (roasted suckling pig) is prepared many different ways in the world, but the Cajun method is the best. Bordelon should know; he is past president of Mansura's annual Cochon de Lait Festival, in which several tons of suckling pigs are cooked on an open fire fed by pecan, oak, and hickory wood. This cooking method allows the grease to drip and the skin to become cracklin' crisp.

A *cochon de lait* requires some preparation—and plenty of help. A twenty-to-thirty-pound suckling pig is slaughtered and then placed spread-eagle between two three-by-four-foot sheets of tin roofing material. The well-seasoned carcass is then placed over a smoking bed of logs to be cooked to a honey golden brown. The cooking process takes about five hours. Sometimes the rack is suspended from a tree limb and is cooked in the indirect convection heat produced by sandwiching the carcass between the matching sheets of tin roofing.

This unique cooking process is an old Cajun tradition. How did it begin?

For families struggling with the devastating effects of the Civil War and Reconstruction era, economic recovery was the first priority. Many farmers consequently increased their acreage under cultivation and began to raise larger numbers of cattle and hogs. The large number of tenant farmers in the local population, however, had fewer resources with which to begin life anew. Lacking money to buy land of their own, these tenant farmers allowed their cattle and hogs to roam the hardwoods freely, gleaning the mast crops and undergrowth for subsistence. These animals fared well because of the ready availability of acorns, pecans, grass, and brierd. During the spring the animals were corralled in slit-railed pens. There the animals were branded, doctored, and returned to the fertile hardwood forests.

The hog pens were really a trap to corner these free-spirited beasts. Dogs like the Catahoula Cur were trained to entice the lead boar to chase them into fifty-by-fifty-foot camouflaged enclosures. Running through the narrow entrance the angered lead hog was invariably followed by the rest of the herd which, in turn, was followed by other Catahoula dogs. Once the hogs were

**155**

penned, the agile canines ran to the opposite side of the pin and then jumped out, leaving the confused swine captured. During the fall the herd was corralled again to be culled and marketed. Riding on horseback, neighbors worked their hogs together. They stayed in the woods for days until the job was done. The reward for this hard work was the roasting of suckling pigs over open fires *(cochon de lait)*. Framed by the woods, lighted by the moon and stars, and warmed by homemade wine or liquor, the merry workers relaxed as the pigs slowly roasted over the fire. An accordion and a fiddle competed with the sounds of a hoot owl as these Cajuns and their neighbors passed a good time.

# Cajun MEN COOK
## BEEF, PORK & LAMB

# BEEF, PORK AND LAMB

# EWING'S BRISKET

3 pounds boneless top
brisket, well trimmed of
fat
1 heaping tablespoon curing
salt, per pound
3 tablespoons coarsely
ground black pepper, more
if you like hot food

2-3 crushed bay leaves
2 teaspoons thyme
10 cloves sliced garlic
2 tablespoons wine or
water, optional

Pat the curing salt into both sides of meat (do not rub in). Add other seasoning, dividing between both sides of meat. Let marinate in glass or pottery container, well covered for 5 days. Turn twice a day. A zip-lock bag works well. After 5 days, place in a cooling pot with water to cover. Simmer for 3 hours or until tender. This liquid is usually too pepper hot to boil the vegetables like potatoes, carrots and cabbage. The accompanying veggies are good steamed in a little water and served with melted butter.

# LAZY CAJUN BRISKET

brisket (any size)
salt, red pepper and black
pepper to taste
1 tablespoon garlic powder

2 tablespoons onion flakes
1 tablespoon liquid smoke
1 pint barbecue sauce

Wash brisket and trim excess fat. Remove all large pieces of fat, but leave some for moistness and flavor. Next, season brisket with salt, red pepper and black pepper. Then sprinkle garlic powder, approximately 1 tablespoon (on average 8-10 pound brisket) and add onion flakes. Pour liquid smoke over brisket. Pour ½ pint of barbecue sauce in baking pan. Next pour ½ pint of barbecue sauce over the brisket. Seal in foil, absolutely tight and bake at approximately 325°F for 5 hours. Voilà!! Easy tender cooked brisket and no fuss or strain at all!! Let cool for 1 hour or more and when it is room temperature, slice approximately quarter inch slices, making sure you slice with the grain of the meat.

*A 10 pound brisket will feed*
*an average party of 10 to 12 people.*

**159**

## DON'S BARBECUE BRISKET

1 beef brisket, 4-6 pounds
1½ teaspoons salt
1 teaspoon garlic powder

½ teaspoon cayenne red
  pepper
½ teaspoon black pepper
¼ teaspoon thyme

**Marinade:**
½ cup firmly packed dark
  brown sugar
⅓ cup cane syrup
2 tablespoons chili powder
4 tablespoons onions,
  minced
¼ cup red wine vinegar,
  (with garlic preferred)

½ cup unsweetened
  pineapple juice
⅓ tablespoons
  Worcestershire sauce
2 tablespoons hot pepper
  sauce

Season meat with seasoning mix of salt, peppers, garlic powder and thyme. Place in a 13x8½x2 inch glass baking dish. Mix marinade and pour over brisket. Cover and place in refrigerator for a maximum of 7 days and minimum of 2 days. Turn brisket over in marinade every 8 or so hours. Reserve marinade. Grill over coals to brown completely for 1 hour. Place in large disposable roasting aluminum pan. Pour marinade over the top. Seal pan with foil and cook over coals for 2 hours.

*12 servings*

# CRAWBEEF (OR CAJUN SURF AND TURF)

4 8 ounce rib-eyes (or
favorite beef steak)
1 pound crawfish (get extra
fat if available)
½ cup oil
3 tablespoons (heaping)
flour

½ block sweet butter
1 medium onion, chopped
2 green onion tops,
chopped
3 cups water

Sauté onions in butter until onions are soft, add green onions and sauté for 1 minute. Set aside. Add ½ cup of oil to 2½ quart saucepan and heat on a medium high fire. Heat oil until hot, add flour and stir until flour is a dark chocolate color (this is your roux). Add sautéed onions to roux and mix well. Add water, stir well, and heat on medium heat until mixture is consistent, about ½ to ¾ of an hour. Lower fire to low after 20 minutes. Add crawfish (and extra fat) after 20 minutes and cook for remaining 25 minutes.

Steak: Marinate steaks overnight in a covered dish. Add steaks (lightly seasoned) with salt and pepper and cover steaks with Worcestershire sauce. Prior to serving the meal, grill on open fire to taste. Serve steak topped with crawfish and sauce.

# MEXICAN ENCHILADA CASSEROLE

2 pounds ground beef
2 tablespoons oil
1 large onion, chopped
1 large bell pepper, chopped
1 10¾ ounce can enchilada
sauce
1 10¾ ounce can cream of
mushroom soup

1 10¾ ounce can water
4 ounces canned green
peppers, chopped
¼ teaspoon cumin
½ teaspoon garlic powder
1 pound cheddar cheese,
grated
tortilla chips

Sauté onions in hot oil. About 5 minutes. Add meat and brown, about 15 minutes. Add other ingredients and mix well. Line 13½x8½x2 inch baking dish with broken tortillas. Bake 1 hour at 350°F.

*8 servings*

## CAJUN HOT TAMALE PIE

3 pounds ground beef with 20% fat content
1½ pound yellow corn meal
⅓ cup vegetable oil
3 large onions, chopped
1 large bell pepper, chopped
2 stalks celery, chopped
3 green onions with tops, chopped
2 garlic cloves, chopped

4 ounces pure chili powder
3 sprigs parsley, chopped
2 16 ounce cans whole tomato (purée)
2 cubes beef bouillon, dissolved in ½ cup of warm water
salt, red and black pepper to taste
grated cheese (optional)

Brown meat in oil on medium fire. Add onions, celery, bell peppers, tomatoes, garlic, 2 ounces of chili powder, beef bouillon, green onion, parsley and seasonings and simmer for 1 hour. Stir occasionally. Remove juices and oil; retain for further use (about 3 cups). Add water if needed to be sure juice covers ¾ depth of pot.

Mix corn meal with 1 ounce of chili powder in a 3 quart pot. Salt and pepper to taste. Mix meat juices, a little at a time to the cornmeal to prevent lumpy texture. Then pour boiling water until mix is consistency of hot cream of wheat. Place on low heat and cook for 20 minutes. Stir frequently to prevent sticking. Add more water as needed to end up with a fluid consistency of cream of wheat. Add more seasonings and garlic powder to both meat and cornmeal mush to taste.

Place alternate ¾ inch layer of meat and cornmeal mush in an 8 quart baking pan or dish. Start with meat on first layer and cornmeal mush as the top layer. Bake in oven at 350°F for approximately 30 minutes (until there is a brown crust on top). Remove and top with grated cheese of your choice (optional). Keep an eye on the pie to be sure it does not dry out due to dry consistency of mush or over baking. Leave in oven longer if too moist. Can be frozen and cooked as needed.

*12 servings*

**This recipe can be used to make hot tamales by doing the following:**
**1. Cook mush for 10 minutes being sure it is fluid like cold molasses.**
**2. Prepare corn leaves by trimming, removing silk and**

soaking in hot water.

3. Place about 1 tablespoon of mush to 1 heaping teaspoon of meat on corn husk. Roll, fold ends and then stack in a pressure cooker or in a steamer or soup pot with tight lid.

4. Pour meat liquid over tamales.

5. Pressure cook for 20 minutes or steam for 45 minutes.

6. Allow to cool to "warm."

*3 dozen*

## CHILI EL CAJUN

3 pounds ground chuck or turkey
2 large onions, chopped
3 ribs celery, chopped
1 large bell pepper, chopped
1 tablespoon salt
1 teaspoon black pepper
1 tablespoon cumin
1 teaspoon granulated garlic
1 tablespoon oregano (optional)
1 tablespoon paprika
1 tablespoon sugar
1 tablespoon granulated dehydrated chicken bouillon

2 tablespoons parsley (dry or fresh)
1 teaspoon baking soda
2 8 ounce cans tomato sauce
1 10¾ ounce can chicken soup
1 10¾ ounce can chicken broth
3 16 ounce cans re-fried beans
2 ounces chili powder
¼ cup dry sherry wine (optional)
pinch red pepper
4 tablespoons olive oil

Using an 8 quart pan, brown meat. Then add onions, celery and bell pepper. Cook until tender. Gradually add rest of ingredients except baking soda. Let simmer for approximately an hour. Stir as needed. Add baking soda and cook 10 minutes or until bubbles dissipate. If chili is too thick, add water. If too thin, thicken with 2 tablespoons corn starch dissolved in ½ cup of water. Cook 10 more minutes until chili thickens.

*8 servings*

**This is definitely a 4-star chili. The refried beans add a creamy texture which delights the palate. Excellent with Cajun potato salad, or cole slaw. Serve with Mexican corn bread. (Optional: Grate sharp cheddar cheese into hot bowl of chili. As a family stretcher, serve over rice.)**

## EWING'S CABBAGE ROLLS

1 head cabbage
2 cans tomato sauce
2 pounds ground meat
1⅓ cups wet corn meal
2 cups onions, chopped fine
½ bell pepper, chopped fine

4 buds garlic, chopped fine
1 tablespoon oil
1 tablespoon chili powder
salt and pepper to taste
½ cup parsley
2 eggs, mixed well

Parboil cabbage leaves for 26 rolls. Mix all of the above ingredients very well. Roll in cabbage leaves and arrange in pot. Sprinkle salt, pepper, chili powder and oil on each layer of rolls. Pour cup (tomato can) of water and a can of tomato sauce. Put on a slow fire. After 1 hour add another can of tomato sauce. Cook 1½ to 2 hours longer. Cool slowly.

*26 rolls*

## CABBAGE ROLLS (OVEN STYLE)

1 large head of cabbage (to
   provide 8 large leaves)
boiling water
2 pounds ground meat
   (beef)

½ cup uncooked rice
2 eggs, beaten
1 large onion, finely cut
season to taste
beef Dolmades Sauce

Core large cabbage, remove 8 leaves or 16 small. Trim off thick parts of leaves and cover in boiling water and let stand for 5 minutes. Meanwhile, mix together ground beef, rice, eggs, onions and seasoning. Remove leaves from water and drain. Place equal amounts of mixture on leaves. Fold. Fold back of cabbage first, then 2 sides. Once again from back place in baking pot. Place cabbage rolls seam side down. Pour Beef Dolmades Sauce on top of cabbage rolls. Cover and bake in preheated 375°F oven for 1 hour. Remove cover and bake ½ hour longer, keep basting with sauce.

**Beef Dolmades Sauce:**
3 8 ounce cans tomato
   sauce
1 cup beef bouillon or broth
1 small green pepper, finely
   cut

⅓ cup sugar
1 large onion, finely cut
3 to 4 celery stalks, cut fine
1 tablespoon parsley flakes
season to taste

Mix thoroughly. Pour over cabbage rolls.

## TRADITIONAL CAJUN MEALS

In rural Acadiana, throughout the first half of the twentieth century, meals were geared to the agrarian work schedules of the families' farm workers. Breakfast was usually light, consisting of cornbread or couche-couche, milk, and sometimes preserves. Lunch, on the other hand, was the principal meal of the day. The noontime meal usually consisted of rice and brown gravy, smothered beef or pork, and seasonal vegetables. Supper (dinner) often included leftovers (if available) or cornbread and milk.

## BOEUF EN DAUBE

2 pounds round steak
4 tablespoons flour
½ teaspoon red pepper
6 strips bacon
1 clove garlic, crushed
1 ounce brandy or whiskey
1 cup beef bouillon
1 cup dry red wine
¼ cup dry red wine

6 medium carrots
2 large or 3 or 4 small onions
3 peppercorns
4 whole cloves
2 teaspoons chopped or dry parsley
¼ teaspoon each marjoram and thyme

Cut steak into 1½ inch cubes. Roll in flour. Salt and pepper mixed. Brown bacon in heavy skillet. Before it gets crisp, remove to large casserole, cut in 1 inch pieces. Brown garlic in bacon fat. Add beef and brown well quickly. Pour brandy over and burn off. Remove to casserole. In remaining fat, put one cup bouillon and one cup wine, bring to boil and scrape bottom and sides of pan. Pour gravy over meat. Add the vegetables — carrots cut in 1 or 2 inch lengths and onions quartered. Last add ¼ cup wine and seasonings. Cover tightly and leave in 300°F oven for 2 hours. This is good hot or cold. If intended to serve hot, add about ½ hour before serving, cooked and quartered potatoes, or about enough to serve 8. Salt and pepper these after placing in casserole.

# MARIO'S WOOD CHIP BEEF

2 pounds round steak,
  sliced into ¼ inch strips
½ cup flour
1 teaspoon salt
¼ cup butter

2 cans mushrooms
1 cup canned tomatoes
1 bay leaf
1 cup red wine

Dredge meat in seasoned flour and brown in butter in heavy pan. Add tomatoes and mushrooms and cook a few minutes longer. Add red wine. Transfer to a 1½ quart casserole dish. Cover and bake for 1 to 1½ hours at 350°F.

*4-6 servings*

*This dish will put you to sleep after you've cut down a big tree. It will feed 4 to 6 normal people, but if lumberjacks are present, double the recipe.*

# ROMA MEAT ROLL

1½ pounds ground beef (or
  use part ground pork)
2 eggs
¼ cup cracker crumbs
½ cup finely chopped
  onions
1 teaspoon salt

½ teaspoon oregano
⅛ teaspoon black pepper
2 cups shredded Mozzarella
  cheese (2-4 ounce
  packages)
2 8 ounce cans tomato
  sauce with cheese, divided

Combine ground meat, eggs, cracker crumbs, onion, salt, oregano, pepper and ⅓ cup of tomato sauce with cheese. Keep remaining tomato sauce. Mix well and shape into a flat rectangle (about 10x12 inch) on wax paper. Sprinkle Mozzarella evenly over meat. Roll up like a jelly roll and press ends of roll to seal. Place in shallow baking pan. Bake in a 350°F preheated oven for 1 hour. Drain off excess fat. Pour remaining tomato sauce over the loaf and bake an additional 15 minutes.

*6 servings*

# BEEF STROGANOFF

2 pounds beef round steak
  cut in long narrow strips
6 tablespoons flour
1½ teaspoon salt (1 for
  dredging and ½ for
  mixture)
½ teaspoon black pepper (¼
  for dredging and ¼ for
  mixture)

bacon drippings
2 cups water
2 teaspoons dry mustard
1 4 ounce can mushrooms
1 onion, sliced
1 cup sour cream

Dredge the meat strips in a mixture of flour, salt and pepper. Brown the meat in a small amount of bacon drippings. Add the water, dry mustard, salt, pepper, mushrooms and sliced onion. Cover and cook over simmer heat for one hour or until meat is tender. Stir occasionally. Make paste of 2 tablespoons of flour and 2 tablespoons water and slowly add to the meat mixture, stirring constantly to prevent lumping. Simmer until gravy is thick and smooth. Stir in 1 cup sour cream and bring to boiling over very low heat. Do not boil mixture, or it will curdle. Serve with hot, fluffy rice.

*4-5 servings*

# ED'S CAJUN MEATBALLS AND SPAGHETTI

½ pound ground round
½ pound ground beef
1 cup French bread crumbs
(finely ground)
2 eggs
1 teaspoon salt
¼ cup finely chopped onion

2 cloves garlic (finely
chopped)
2 tablespoons Parmesan
cheese
¾ teaspoon red pepper
Creole seasoning to taste
1 6 ounce can large button
mushrooms

Mix above ingredients in a large mixing bowl, form into balls placing a button mushroom in the center of each meatball. Put the 10 meatballs on a large cookie sheet; brown at 400°F in the oven for 30-40 minutes until dark brown.

**Tomato Sauce:**
1 large onion (finely
chopped)
2 cloves garlic (finely
chopped)
2 6 ounce cans tomato
paste
2 15 ounce cans tomato
sauce
½ 10 ounce can tomatoes
with chilies

1 large bell pepper (finely
chopped)
3 tablespoons parsley
(finely chopped)
2 teaspoons sugar
3 tablespoons peanut oil
2 6 ounce cans sliced
mushrooms

Lightly brown onion, garlic, bell pepper in peanut oil (about 15 minutes). Add tomato paste, tomato sauce, tomatoes with chilies and 3 cups of water and season to taste (Creole seasoning). Add sugar and meatballs to sauce and cook on low fire for at least 3 hours. Add more water as needed if sauce gets too thick. About 20 minutes before serving, add sliced mushrooms and parsley. Cook one large pack (32 ounce) of angel hair spaghetti. Serve with hot garlic French bread and Italian green salad. Enjoy!

*Will make approximately 10 large meatballs*          *4-6 servings*

## PEPPERED BEEF (AMAZINGLY TENDER)

| | |
|---|---|
| 1 4-5 pound brisket beef (trim fat and tenderize) | ¼ cup coarsely cracked black pepper |

Spread pepper on waxed paper. Place beef on pepper and press beef firmly into pepper. Repeat the above to cover all sides of beef.

**Marinade:**

| | |
|---|---|
| ⅔ cup soy sauce | ⅓ cup cider vinegar |
| 1 tablespoon catsup | 1 large clove crushed garlic |
| 1 tablespoon Worcestershire sauce | |

Combine all ingredients and pour over beef in shallow pan. Refrigerate overnight, turning beef at least twice. When ready to cook, remove beef from marinade and wrap securely in heavy foil. Place in shallow pan and bake at 300°F for 3-3½ hours. Excellent served hot or cold, sliced thin - ¼ inch or less. Variation: 4-6 pound rib-eye of beef - same procedure and recipe for medium rare. Cook for 1½ hour at 300°F or use thermometer when cooked as desired, remove foil and place rib-eye under broiler for 1-2 minutes per side.

*8 servings*

## MEAL-IN-ONE FOR RICE COOKER

| | |
|---|---|
| 3-4 red potatoes unpeeled cut in ½ inch slices | 2-3 links smoked sausage cut in 1 inch slices |
| small head of cabbage cut in wedges | 1 can tomatoes with chilies or 1 package of onion soup mix |
| 3-4 medium onions cut in half | |

Place in layers into rice cooker using steamer plate. Use ½ cup of water under plate. Cook for 40 minutes.

*4-6 servings*

# STUFFED MANICOTTI

1 box Manicotti pasta
1 pound bulk raw sausage
1 pound ground meat
2 chopped boiled eggs
1 package frozen spinach
(thawed)
6 ounces grated Parmesan
cheese
6 ounces grated Romano
cheese
2 tablespoons olive oil

1 onion, chopped
5 toes garlic, chopped
1 bell pepper, chopped
3 green onions, chopped
1 tablespoon parsley
1 teaspoon oregano
½ teaspoon garlic powder
½ teaspoon mint
salt and pepper
1 package Provolone cheese

Boil Manicotti pasta to package directions. Set aside. Brown sausage and ground meat, drain well. In a large mixing bowl combine ground meat, sausage, boiled eggs, spinach, Parmesan and Romano Cheese, chopped onion, garlic, bell pepper, green onions, parsley, oregano, garlic powder, mint, salt and pepper and mix all ingredients well. Stuff pasta with mix. Oil a large baking dish (glass is best). Line pasta in dish and cover with sliced Provolone cheese. Cover generously with your favorite spaghetti sauce. Bake at 350°F for 45 minutes. Serve with garlic bread.

# PORK IN WINE

1 large onion, chopped
½ cup parsley
1 cup Italian bread crumbs

white wine to taste
2 pounds seasoned pork
1 cup chicken broth

Place seasoned pork in casserole dish. Add chopped onions and parsley; add bread crumbs, then wine. Bake at 400°F for 10 minutes. Add broth; bake at 350°F for 50 minutes.

*4-6 servings*

# NATCHITOCHES HOT MEAT PIE

2 tablespoons flour
1 tablespoon bacon fat
½ pound ground beef
1½ pound round pork
3 cups onion, chopped fine
1 cup green onions, chopped fine
1 cup bell pepper, chopped fine

3 tablespoons parsley, chopped fine
3 cloves garlic, minced
1½ teaspoon salt
½ teaspoon black pepper
⅛ teaspoon cayenne red pepper

Pastry:
4 cups sifted flour
2 teaspoons baking powder
½ cup melted shortening

2 eggs, beaten
¼ cup of milk

Filling: Make a roux of flour and shortening. Add all remaining ingredients, cover and cook on low fire for 30 minutes. Drain and cool while making pastry.

Pastry: Sift flour and baking powder together. Add shortening, then eggs. Add milk to make a stiff dough. Roll very thin, about ⅛ inch thick. Use saucer to make circles of dough. Fill ½ full with meat mixture. Fold dough over and dampen edges with water and crimp with fork. Fry in deep fat until golden brown.

*15 pies*

# BLACK IRON POTS

In Cajun cooking, the utensils are almost as important as the ingredients. Most Cajun cooks have favorite pots and pans, special knives, a badly stained apron, an old plank used as a cutting board, and other assorted "essential" cooking items. Of course, one of the most important items is the black iron pot usually cast iron and almost always with a coating that could best be described as the ghost of many good meals past.

Black iron pots evolved from the use of fireplaces equipped with hook devices that swung the pot over the fire. Some of these pots had feet and flat, slightly depressed lids. Such pots were usually used when cooking out in the woods over open camp fires. The pot was placed directly over hot coals (the reason for the feet) and in some cases, hot coals were placed in the depression on the lid in order to bake biscuits or cornbread.

Stainless steel and aluminum pots have largely displaced their black iron counterparts; however, most Cajun cooks have the old cast-iron stand-by waiting and ready for that special gumbo. Somehow, the new pots, especially those with teflon coatings, just do not cook as well. Some old-timers actually think that iron pots are healthy because minute particles of iron are sloughed and eventually end up as an iron supplement to the diet.

The care of a black iron pot is considered very important. A new pot has to be "seasoned" (broken in) by heating it to a high temperature, letting it cool slightly, and then coating it with cooking oil. The oil is wiped off—not washed off—and the pot is left to season. This procedure is often repeated several times before the pot is ready for serious cooking. Cleaning is another story. Abrasives and steel wool are never used because they affect the seasoning or coating process. A small amount of detergent and a rag are usually used, and the pot is rinsed and heated slightly to remove the moisture, then recoated with oil and put away for future use. Experience has shown that the ugliest black pot is the one that cooks best.

# MONTESANTO'S VEAL/CRAWFISH FETTUCCINE

1½ pounds veal cutlets, sliced thinly
2 large eggs
½ cup milk
1 teaspoon salt, or to taste
½ teaspoon fresh ground black pepper
2 cups Italian bread crumbs
½ cup flour
1¼ pounds butter
2 pounds crawfish meat
2 small bell peppers, chopped fine
3 large onions, chopped fine
4 cloves garlic, chopped fine
2 packages Alfredo Fettuccine Mix

On medium heat, in a 4 quart saucepan melt 1 pound of butter and sauté onions, bell peppers, and garlic until onions are opaque. Set aside. Bread veal cutlets by first dipping in the bowl mix of eggs, milk, salt, and pepper; then place meat in a flat dish mix of 2 cups bread crumbs and ½ cup of flour, salt, and pepper to taste; pat on both sides to assure cutlets are well coated with crumbs. Set aside. To prepare fettuccine noodles, follow instructions on package. While noodles are boiling, heat sautéed vegetables; add and sauté crawfish for about 15 minutes. Serve warm. Place a veal cutlet on each plate; serve a portion of fettuccine next to meat; top both with the rich crawfish sauce.

*6 servings*

To complete the entrée, add a good Italian salad, toasted garlic bread and red wine.

# BOB'S VEAL PARMIGIANA

4 veal cutlets, ¼ inch thick
  (about 1 pound)
1 cup dried bread crumbs
1 teaspoon salt
⅛ teaspoon black pepper
2 tablespoons Parmesan
  cheese
2 eggs, beaten

3-5 tablespoons butter or
  margarine
tomato sauce (recipe
  follows)
1 8 ounce package
  Mozzarella cheese, grated
¼ cup Parmesan cheese

Prepare cutlets. Mix together bread crumbs, salt and black pepper. Beat 2 tablespoons Parmesan cheese into the eggs. Dip cutlets into eggs, then bread crumbs. Repeat to coat twice. Cover and refrigerate for 30 minutes. Melt the butter in a skillet. Sauté the cutlets, without crowding, about 10 minutes or until brown on both sides, adding more butter as needed. When tender, spoon some of the tomato sauce over each cutlet. Top with Mozzarella cheese. Cover and cook 5 minutes longer or until cheese is melted. Sprinkle with the ¼ cup Parmesan cheese.

**The chilling of the breaded cutlets keeps the breading intact during frying.**

**Tomato Sauce:**
1 onion, chopped
1 clove garlic, minced or
  pressed
2 tablespoons oil
1 1 pound can tomatoes

¼ cup tomato paste
¾ teaspoon salt
2 teaspoons basil and
  oregano leaves, dried

Sauté onion and garlic in oil. Stir in can tomatoes, tomato paste, salt, basil and oregano leaves. Simmer, stirring frequently, 20 to 30 minutes until thickened.

# MAYOR BERTHELOT'S JAMBALAYA

3 pounds lean pork, 1 inch cubes

2 pounds mixed smoked sausage, diced

½ cup cooking oil

2 teaspoons granulated sugar

1 bunch shallots with tops; chopped fine (separate greens from bottom)

5 large onions, chopped fine

4 stalks celery, chopped fine

1 large bell pepper, chopped fine

5 teaspoons black pepper

3 teaspoons hot sauce

3 teaspoons salt, or to taste

4½ cups long grain rice

9 cups water

Brown sausage in cooking oil in 12 quart iron pot, about 10 minutes on medium heat. Remove and set aside. Brown pork in oil residue until it begins to brown; add sausage and cook on medium heat uncovered until golden brown. About 20 minutes. Remove and set aside. Add chopped onions and cook until dark brown; sauté for 12 minutes covered on low heat. Add 9 cups of water and all seasonings; add more seasonings and salt to be sure water is salty as rice will absorb salt. Bring to a good boil then cut off fire and let set for 25 minutes. Remove excess oil which comes to the top. Return to fire and bring to boil again. Add rice and stir until water becomes opaque and thick; stir gently not to break rice. Cover with tight lid and simmer on low fire for 15 minutes, or until rice is cooked. Gently fluff rice and add onion tops. Do not stir again. Cover and let sit 15 minutes and then serve.

*14 servings*

## HONEY-SOY SPARERIBS

4 pounds fresh pork
  spareribs
1½ cups beef broth bouillon
⅓ cup soy sauce
3 tablespoons cider vinegar
2 tablespoons sherry

1 tablespoon sugar
1 teaspoon salt
2 teaspoons ground ginger
¼ teaspoon garlic powder
green onion tassels (to show
  green and white of onion)

Place spareribs in 13½x9½x2 inch baking dish. Mix all ingredients except onion tassels in a small bowl. Rub marinade well on spareribs, pouring excess onto the meat. Cover and refrigerate for at least 6 hours. Remove meat from marinade; reserve marinade. Arrange ribs meaty sides up in single layer on rack in foil-lined pan. Cover and cook in 350°F oven for 45 minutes. Brush ribs with marinade. Cook uncovered, brushing occasionally with marinade, until tender, about 50 minutes. Garnish with green onion tassels.

*4 servings*

**Add yams and fried rice to help complete the menu.**

## OSSOBUCO (ITALIAN VEAL OR BEEF SHANKS)

4 tablespoons olive oil
6 shanks cut into 3 inch
  pieces
1 cup chopped onions
1 large clove garlic,
  chopped
2 cups Italian style
  tomatoes

4 tablespoons margarine
½ cup all purpose flour
½ cup chopped celery
1 cup chopped carrots
1½ cup Madeira wine
oregano and sweet basil to
  taste
1½ cup chicken stock

Heat margarine and oil in Dutch oven. Dust shanks in flour and brown on all sides. Remove shanks, add vegetables and sauté until soft. Add tomatoes, chicken stock, wine and seasonings. Return shanks to Dutch oven and cook for about 2 hours, stirring occasionally. Serve over pasta.

*6 servings*

# PORK WITH LEMON

2 pounds pork boneless
  shoulder
3 cloves garlic, chopped
2 tablespoons lemon juice
1 tablespoon olive oil
1 teaspoon salt
¼ teaspoon ground cumin

½ teaspoon ground cayenne
  red pepper
1 tablespoon olive oil
½ cup dry red wine
½ cup pitted ripe olives
garnish, slices of lemon and
  orange wedges

Cut pork into ¾ inch pieces. Toss pork, garlic, lemon juice, table-spoon of oil, the salt, cumin, wine, and red peppers in glass or plastic bowl. Cover and refrigerate for at least 8 hours. Stir occasionally. Remove pork from marinade: reserve any remaining marinade. Heat 1 tablespoon oil in skillet until hot. Cook and stir pork in oil over medium heat until liquid has evaporated and pork is brown; drain. Add water and reserved marinade. Cover and simmer until pork is tender; about 30 minutes. Add more water if needed. Stir in olives. Serve and garnish with orange and lemon wedges.

*6 servings*

**The lemon in this recipe marries the other seasonings into the meat. The result is a very delectable pork dish.**

**Serve over rice or toasted garlic French bread.**

# LEG OF LAMB

3 to 4 pound leg of lamb
salt and pepper - lots
2 cloves garlic
¼ bell pepper

lemon peel
4 ounces butter or oleo
1 large onion
½ or 1 small bell pepper

Sliver garlic, bell pepper and lemon peel and insert in leg of lamb. Refrigerate overnight. Next day, set oven at 400°F; salt and pepper leg of lamb generously. Place in roaster with 4 ounces butter in pan. Heat in hot oven for 30 minutes. Brown on both sides. Add chopped onion and sauté in pan (may have to add very small amount of water to keep onions from burning.) When transparent, add chopped bell pepper - 1½ cups water, cover. Lower heat to 350°F and bake until done. Thicken gravy in pan with flour. Season and serve with mint jelly and rice.

## PORK CHOPS GLAZED WITH CHEESE

4 loin pork chops, about 1½
  pounds
salt and freshly ground
  pepper to taste
1 tablespoon vegetable oil
¼ pound grated Gruyère or
  Swiss cheese
1 tablespoon imported
  mustard (Dijon)

1 tablespoon heavy cream
½ teaspoon finely chopped
  garlic
1 tablespoon finely chopped
  chives
1 egg yolk
2 tablespoons dry white
  wine
2 tablespoons water

Sprinkle chops with salt and pepper. Heat the oil in a heavy skillet and add the chops. Cook until nicely browned on one side, turn and continue cooking until browned and cooked through. Preheat broiler. As the chops cook, blend the remainder of the ingredients, except the wine and water. When the chops are cooked, place in broiling pan and smear one side with equal portions of the cheese mixture, smoothing it over the chop. Run the chops under the broiler until the topping is browned and nicely glazed. Meanwhile, pour off the fat from the skillet in which the chops were cooked. Add the wine to the skillet, stirring, and add the water. Bring to a boil. Stir to dissolve the brown particles that cling to the bottom and sides of the skillet. Pour the hot sauce over the chops and serve.

*4 servings*

## BOB BULLOCK'S ITALIAN SAUSAGE

25 pounds ground pork
6 ounces table salt
3 ounces ground fennel

1½ ounces black pepper
1½ ounces chopped red
  pepper

Thoroughly mix, cover and allow to stand overnight. If you refrigerate, the sausage will not turn out as good. In selecting hanks of casings, be sure that they are fresh. Merely smell them to be sure that they are not old and rancid. Don't even think about using anything but natural casings. Using a sausage-making press, fill the casings with the mixture. The sausages can be refrigerated if you plan on using them quickly. But they can be frozen for long-term storage. Because you have made sausage in this manner, you must thoroughly cook the sausages before eating them.

## BOB BULLOCK'S REGULAR SAUSAGE

2 pounds salt (salt used for either canning or cooking)
10 heaped teaspoons pepper
40 pounds beef and 60 pounds of pork

1 haze mustard seed
1 toe garlic
2 hanks casings (be sure they are fresh and not old and rancid)

Thoroughly mix the ingredients. Cover and allow to stand overnight. If you refrigerate, the sausage will not turn out as good. Using a sausage-making press, fill the casings with the mixture. The sausages can be refrigerated if you plan on using them quickly. But they can be frozen for long-term storage. Because you have made sausage in this manner, you must thoroughly cook the sausages before eating them.

*approximately 100 pounds of sausage*

## SWEET AND SOUR OVEN BARBECUED SPARE RIBS

3 to 4 seasoned spareribs
1 cup tomato sauce
4 tablespoons honey
2 cloves garlic
1 teaspoon dry mustard

2 teaspoons chili powder
2 teaspoons oregano
2 tablespoons lemon juice
1½ teaspoon ground ginger
2 tablespoons soy sauce

Have butcher cut slab of seasoned ribs in half perpendicular to rib bones. Cut ribs in single small serving pieces and place, in single layers, in bottom of large Pyrex (13x9x1½ inch) dish. Mix together all remaining ingredients and pour over ribs. Cover well and marinate in refrigerator overnight, turning several times. Remove cover and place in 350°F oven for 1½ hours. During the final hour of cooking, turn and baste frequently.

*4-6 servings*

## CATALIAN MEAT SAUCE

1 pound fresh pork sausage, loose, Italian preferred
2 pounds ground beef
4 large onions, chopped
4 cloves garlic, minced
1 cup onion tops, chopped
1 cup celery, chopped
1 cup parsley, chopped
1 8 ounce can mushrooms, stems and pieces
3 15 ounce cans tomato sauce
1 fifth (750 ml) dry red wine, such as Chianti
2 teaspoons salt
1 teaspoon sage
½ teaspoon thyme
1 teaspoon rosemary
½ teaspoon marjoram
½ teaspoon black pepper
⅛ teaspoon red pepper

Brown meat in large saucepan. Drain off fat, add onions, celery, garlic and mushrooms. Cook on low heat until onions are opaque. Add all other ingredients and simmer for 3 hours or until sauce is thickened. Add onion tops and parsley. Serve over spaghetti. Sprinkle Parmesan cheese on each plate served.

*8 servings*

# LAGNIAPPE SECTION
# BEEF

## MAKING BOUDIN

### (Cajun Rice Sausage)

According to the punch line of an old Acadiana joke, a Cajun seven-course meal consists of one pound of boudin and a six pack of beer. This punch line is so close to the truth that we felt duty bound to include this section on boudin making. Boudin served hot or cold in party links or as fried boudin balls make hardy hors d'oeuvres. Here is what you will need to make this delicacy:

**10 pounds pork roast cut into 1½ inch steaks**
**1 pound pork liver**
**4 bunches shallots chopped fine**
**1 bunch parsley chopped fine**

**30 tablespoons Cajun seasoning mix in water to cover the meat**
**6¼ cups fancy medium grain rice (raw)**
**8 cups meat broth (from the boiled pork)**
**15 feet hog casing size 35 to 38 millimeter**

The best cut of pork for boudin is shoulder roast with the rind. Have the butcher cut the roast on his meat saw retaining the bone dust. (The rind and the bone dust help set the ingredients when they cool.) Place meat and liver in pot and cover with seasoned water. Bring to a boil and lower heat to simmer. Cook for 2½ hours or until meat falls from the bones. When done, remove meat and allow to cool retaining the broth on simmer. Debone the meat and discard the bones. While meat is cooking prepare fifty ounces of rice. This equals ten rice cooker cups or 6¼ standard measuring cups. Do not add salt to the rice. Cook rice in a rice cooker or steamer to a "fluffy" condition.

Chop the shallots and the parsley fine—including stems—and set aside.

Wash the hog casing and set it aside. Grind liver and pork meat once through a ⅜ inch sieve. After the rice is cooked put it into a large mixing container. Pour the shallots and the parsley into the simmering broth. Turn off heat and after one minute remove shallots, parsley, and any small meat solids with a screening spoon and scatter on the surface of the rice.

Taste the broth for seasoning. If you prefer more pepper, add red cayenne one tablespoon at a time until it suits your taste.

Gently mix the meat and the rice by hand and slowly add eight cups of the seasoned broth all the while mixing ingredients. Mixture should be moist but not soggy. You may have broth remaining in the pot, if so use it as stock.

Stuff casing as described in the selection entitled Smoke Sausage. When casing has been stuffed it is usually twisted into eight- or ten-inch links and kept refrigerated. Although sometimes eaten cold, it is best served warm. It can be warmed in a microwave oven or by merely submerging it in simmering water.

If you desire keeping boudin more than three days, freeze it. The boudin will retain its flavor in the frozen state for about three months.

## CRACKLIN MAKING

Cajun cracklins (pork rinds) are the best in the world. Making cracklins, although involved, is not particularly difficult. Be warned however, that this procedure is not for beginners. Even old hands at cracklin-making occasionally turn out a less-than-perfect batch. It is, nevertheless, fun to try your hand at cracklin making. The recipe and instructions set out below will provide less adventurous readers with an insight into the production of these Cajun munchies.

The best cracklin is produced from green pork bellies. The fat-layered meat is located over the hog's rib cage and has five distinct layers of tissue. Starting from the rib cage is a ⅛-inch layer of lean meat, then a thin layer of fat followed by more meat, then a ¾-inch layer of fat, and finally the rind. Green pork bellies can be purchased from meat wholesalers in fifty-pound boxes, containing four-to-five slabs per box. Begin by freezing each slab and then cutting the meat into 1½-inch squares with a meat saw.

A big iron pot heated by wood fire or a butane gas heat source are needed for cooking the cracklins. Such a rig makes it easy to control temperatures. The iron pot reduces bottom burning during the cooking stage.

Mix one-half gallon of pig lard or oil with one quart of water for every ten pounds of pork fat. The water helps render the fat and makes the cracklins more tender. To begin the cooking procedure, put the chunks of fat into the pot along with the oil and water. Cook over medium heat until the liquid reaches 220°F. Stir gently, but sparingly, for approximately eight minutes to prevent the fat from sticking to the pot. Look for dirty gray suds to begin forming around the edges of the pot. This indicates that, although the meat is warming up, the fat is not frying. A brownish ring should appear about five minutes later, indicating that the fat is being rendered and that it is not sticking to the pot. Increase the heat to 250°F. Eight minutes later the brownish ring is replaced with a white, sudsy foam. The cracklins at this point will look brownish/gray. Lower the heat to 200°F and cook for about 40 minutes, until white suds appear. Test the cracklins for firmness by hitting bloating cracklins with a paddle blade. Cracklins at this stage of the cooking process should produce a sound similar to striking a wooden door. You may remove a few cracklins from the pot and check to see if they are rubbery, not mushy. Look also for air blisters on the rind. If the cracklins exhibit these traits, bring the pot to a full boil at 350°F. Meanwhile, stir the cracklins with a paddle and periodically lift the cracklins into the air to pop the rind. Also add four or five ice cubes. The ice will sink to the bottom of the pot, melt, and cause the hot lard to explode the rind of the cracklin—an effect which will help guarantee tenderness and crispness. Remove finished cracklins and place them in cardboard boxes or on wrapping paper to drain. Season them while hot with the universal Cajun seasoning mixture. If you have followed the foregoing procedure perfectly, your cracklins will be crisp and delicious. As an extra bonus, peel and cut Louisiana yams into half-inch slices. Fry in the hot lard and then drain on absorbent paper. Sprinkle with cinnamon sugar mix while hot.

## TASSO

Tasso, used as a flavoring agent in other dishes including gumbos, beans, and soups, might best be described as Cajun ham.

Use it sparingly, for it does not take much to produce the smoked flavor you seek. Boston butt roast is the best pork cut for tasso production. Have the butcher slice the meat into ½ or ¾ inch slices. Marinate ten pounds of sliced meat for seventy-two hours in a mixture consisting of ten tablespoons of basic Cajun seasoning mix, two level teaspoons of sodium nitrite, and sixteen ounces of water. Ensure that meat is completely submerged in marinade. If more marinade is needed use the same proportions as above. After seventy-two hours remove meat, pat dry with paper towels and rub on dry Cajun seasoning mix. Hang meat in smoke chamber allowing sufficient space between slices to permit free flow of smoke and heat between individual slices.

## JERKY MAKING

Jerky is smoked and seasoned strips of beef much favored by hunters and fishermen because they can be carried in a nap sack and eaten as snacks. The best cut of beef to use is bottom round. The roast should be stiffened by chilling and then sliced into ³⁄₁₆ inch slices. The slices are then trimmed into 1 inch wide strips so that the meat is ready for seasoning. Jerky is more highly seasoned than other smoked meat, although the ratio of two level measuring teaspoons of sodium nitrite to ten pounds of meat is the same; three level tablespoons of Cajun seasoning mix is used for each pound of meat. To determine the amount of water to be used, put the meat into a marinating pot and cover it with water. Remove the meat from the container and put it in the Cajun seasoning mixture at the rate of three tablespoons full per pound of meat. After stirring the mixture well, return the meat to the container and marinate it for at least seventy-two hours. To obtain different flavors, add Worcestershire sauce, brown sugar, pineapple, jellies, Tabasco, or other ingredients to the mix. If you use brown sugar, use one pound of brown sugar to ten pounds of meat. When the marinating process is complete, hang the meat in a smoke chamber and allow it to drip for one hour and then slowly apply heat. Because of the thinness of these beef strips only about two hours of heat will be needed to complete the process. Check to see if the meat is done; a strip should withstand being bent double without breaking and the color on the outside of the meat should be a dark red, while the inside is a dull pink. When the meat reaches this point, reduce the heat to about 110°F and smoke the meat for about one-half hour more. Jerky may be carried on the person and eaten as a snack; however, for long term storage it should be refrigerated properly.

## HEAT SOURCES FOR COOKING

Regardless of what some uninformed people think, Cajuns do have modern appliances. Although a Cajun cook is usually an expert in open-fire cooking over barbecue grills, camp fires, and fireplaces, most Cajun cooking is done on regular stoves. The true Cajun cook prefers a gas range mainly because the stove's heat can be regulated precisely, and the adjustment is virtually instantaneous as compared to the slow reaction of electric stoves. Many Cajun recipes will state "a low fire" which indicates a minute flame pattern. A lot depends on the cook's overall cooking experience as well as his/her experience with a particular stove. Many Cajun cooks continuously scan their stoves, monitoring foods' progress and the flames' status on specific burners.

Though the gas stove reigns supreme in the Cajun kitchen; charcoal grills are the heat source of choice for outdoor cooks, who generally disdain the use of gas grills for barbecues. Very few Cajun cooks will allow anyone else to build their outdoor cooking fires. Barbecues usually begin only after the cook has started his own fire and then determined that the coals are "just right" before putting the food on the grill. Even with modern day charcoal briquettes most cooks have their favorite brand. They have learned from experience the amount of heat the coals omit, how long the temperature, and how soon charcoal must be added. In some cases there is even a preferred fire starting liquid other than the commercial liquid fire starters. One expert barbecue in Cajun country had access to jet fuel and used it very successfully to start his charcoal fires.

Then, there is the butane burner which is normally used for boiling seafood (shrimp, crabs, or crawfish) and also frying large amounts of fresh fish. No matter what the fuel the cook uses it is a good bet the food will be excellent.

# CAJUN MICROWAVE

The Cajun love for cooking good food and having fun doing it encourages local cooks to find new and better ways of preparing food. The Cajun microwave resulted from a search for a new method of cooking pork outdoors in an oven using charcoal or hardwood as a heat source. Typically the Cajun microwave is nothing more than a wooden box (untreated and unpainted), lined with sheet metal or heavy foil. The lid of the box is made of steel and indented 2 to 6 inches to accommodate glowing coals as a heat source. The indented portion fits snugly into the open box. Handles are installed on the lid to allow easy lifting to check the contents. Usually the bottom of the box has a drain of some sort to drain off juices from the food. In addition, the meat is placed on a rack to facilitate the insertion and removal of the contents. The overall size of the Cajun microwave varies from a small one to cook a roast up to those large enough to roast a whole suckling pig. The device's design allows heat to radiate downward and trap moisture while cooking imparts a special flavor to the contents. While commonly used for pork, other meats and fish can be cooked to perfection in a Cajun microwave.

## BUILDING AND USING A CAJUN MICROWAVE

The Cajun tradition of culinary innovation is clearly evident is this portable roasting oven. The Cajun microwave relies on convection heat for cooking meat. To build a unit capable of accommodating a small pig, use the materials set out below: 1) A fire tray made of cast iron or wood covered with $\frac{1}{16}$ inch (or thicker) metal. 2) The body of the oven fabricated with oak boards or $\frac{3}{4}$ inch marine plywood. The box's entire interior should be lined with $\frac{1}{32}$ inch (or thicker) aluminum or other sheet metal. A one-half-inch hole must be drilled into the oven's sloping floor to provide a drain for excess liquids generated by the cooking process. A one-half-gallon can must be placed beneath this hole to collect the runoff. 3) Legs made of angle irons or wood. One pair of legs should be $\frac{3}{4}$ inch shorter than the other pair so that the floor will slant to facilitate drainage of excess fluids. 4) A metal grill, which must be placed on the floor of the oven to hold meat for cooking.

To prepare this model of the Cajun microwave for cooking, fill the fire tray (lipped around the edges) with charcoal. Insert the fire tray into the top of the oven. Ignite the charcoal after first inserting into the oven the pre-seasoned pork, turkey, chicken, venison, fish, or other meat that you intend to cook. You can monitor the progress of the cooking by peering through the viewing window.

Here are some helpful hints for new Cajun microwave cooks: 1) Use Cajun Seasoning Mix. It can be mixed with water, and the mixture can then be injected into meat by means of a hypodermic needle. To prevent blockage of openings in the hypodermic needle, make small slits in tough skinned pork or roasts before attempting the injection. The same seasoning mixture can be applied to the exterior of the meat while basting. 2) Open the oven only twice for basting. 3) Half a pig cooks faster than a whole pig of the same weight. 4) Try adding whole potatoes, yams, or carrots to the oven near the end of the baking process for a delightful treat. 5) Always clean the microwave thoroughly after cooking and remove all charcoal from the fire tray.

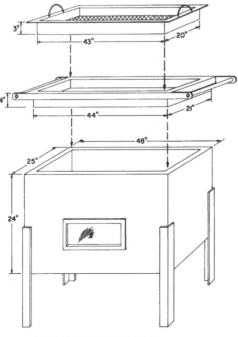

**CAJUN MICROWAVE**

# BARREL SMOKE HOUSE

The Cooperative Extension Services of Louisiana State University and Texas A & M University developed this barrel smoke house diagram. It is simple enough for a novice to build, but effective enough for an experienced camper to use. Check with your local fire marshal before using this device.

This smoker requires a 50-gallon barrel with both ends removed. The can may be used to smoke small quantities of meat or fish. The can must be located at the end of a shallow, sloping, covered trench leading to a small fire pit. The trench can be covered with a 1x10 inch board or an elongated piece of sheet metal. If a board is used, a stone or brick should be placed on top of the fire pit flue to prevent the wood from igniting.

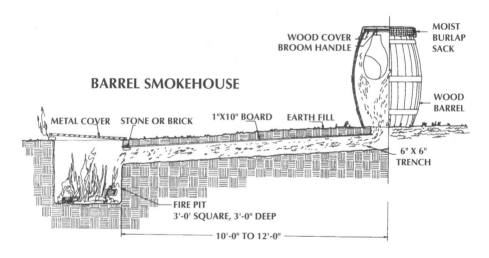

Control the heat generated by the fire by covering the pit with a piece of sheet metal and putting loose dirt around the edges of the cover to reduce the fire's air supply.

Suspend the meat to be smoked from broom handles laid across the top of the barrel. Cover the broom handles with the barrel's wooden cover. Place a moist, clean burlap sack over the top of the barrel and drape the sack over the sides in order to protect the meat inside the smoker.

A box with enclosed sides, but with the top and bottom removed, can be substituted for a barrel. In addition, several layers of burlap sacks can be substituted for a wooden cover. Finally, a stove pipe, a large pipe, or tile can be used as a flue.

Whenever possible, the barrel smoker should be located on a slope so that the flue will have a good pitch from the fire pit to the barrel (or box) smoker.

## PREPARING AND SMOKING MEAT

Smoking any food obviously requires a smokehouse or a smoker of some sort which allows the food being smoked to be hung some distance from the fire in such a way that all of the smoke from burning green or wet wood (preferably pecan, hickory, beach, or oak) will circulate around the food before it is vented out of the smoke chamber. Temperature in the smoke chamber should never exceed 165°F if the fire is located at least 10 feet from the smoke chamber. Because of the relatively low heat level maintained in the smoke chamber, smoking requires considerably more time than other methods of cooking. It also imports an entirely different flavor and color as a result of the smoke being at least equal to heat in the cooking process.

Prepare meat for smoking as follows: for every 10 pounds of meat take 10 tablespoons of basic Cajun seasoning mix and add 2 level teaspoons of sodium nitrite and 16 ounces of water. Sodium nitrite is a preservative and should be used only when smoking meat, fish, or fowl. It will prevent the meat from souring during the relatively long cooking period. It need not be used if smoking is being done in cold winter temperatures. Marinate the meat in this mixture overnight. If meat is in portions thicker than 1 inch then some of the marinade should be injected in the meat using a syringe. Prior to hanging meat in the smoke chamber, pat it dry with paper towels and rub the exterior with dry Cajun seasoning. Hang meat in the smoke chamber.

It will take 3 to 4 hours for the temperature in the smoke chamber to reach 165°F. Once this temperature is reached allow heat to diminish to about 115°F (use an oven thermometer hung along side the meat). The time for the entire process will vary depending on the thickness of the meat being smoked. Smoke meat can be kept refrigerated for up to six weeks without spoiling. It can be frozen but freezing tends to dry it out and to rob it of its flavor.

# CAJUN SMOKED SAUSAGE

Boston butt is the best cut of pork for production of Cajun smoked sausage. Leave the fat cap to provide the proper fat to lean ratio. Remove the bone blade and gland. A good beef/pork mix is twenty percent beef and eighty percent pork.

Grind ten pounds of meat through a ⅜ inch grinder sieve. Add a mixture of ten tablespoons of basic Cajun seasoning mix, two level teaspoons of sodium nitrite and sixteen ounces of water to the ground meat. (Sodium nitrite prevents spoilage during the smoking process.) Run the meat and the seasoning mixture through the grinder again. If you prefer course ground meat remove the blade and the sieve; otherwise the meat will be ground finer. Water keeps the finished product from becoming dry and crumbly. If the mix appears to be to dry add six ounces of water. After thoroughly mixing meat, seasoning mix, and water, fry a small sample and check for taste. If the result is too bland, add more seasoning mix. A touch of sage will also improve the final product.

Wash the sausage casing in fresh water, using thirty-five to thirty-eight millimeter pork casings to produce sausage of one inch diameter.

Use a clean cow horn, funnel, home meat grinder, or commercial sausage stuffer to fill casing with meat. Make sure there are no air pockets in casing as you stuff it; however, "do not pack" the meat into the casing.

If links are desired, run your right hand along the sausage from one end of the sausage to a point about 8 inches from the end and pinch the sausage so that your thumb, forefinger, and middle finger are touching. Using your left hand, grasp the sausage rope about two feet away from your right hand and swing the sausage clockwise about 10 turns (like swinging a jump rope). While still holding the first pinch point with your right hand, slide your left hand toward your right hand to a point eight inches short of the initial pinch and pinch with left hand. Move the right hand to the pinch made by the left hand, and, grasping the pinch, move the left hand back to the left about two feet and swing the rope again, thereby forming the second link. Repeat procedure until the entire length of rope is linked.

Hang the sausage rope in smoked chamber and let drip dry for about one hour. Later heat and smoke as outlined in the section entitled Preparing and Smoking Meat.

# CAJUN FAMILIES GATHERED NEARLY EVERY SUNDAY

Cajun families gathered nearly every Sunday, and the noon meal was usually a treat. Food was often set aside throughout the week for Sunday dinner. Cajun hospitality dictated that anyone present at mealtime be invited to join the family. This was especially true when the visitors were relatives.

Such was the case one Sunday at the J. W. "Pete" Delahoussaye home. Extra guests at the table were usually no problem because a little water could be added to the gumbo, or more rice could be added to the pot, or the roast could be carved a little thinner. Fried chicken, however, posed a different problem, for there were only so many pieces to go around, and the meal couldn't be "stretched."

One fine Sunday, several Delahoussaye cousins arrived shortly before the noontime meal. Therese Delahoussaye made quick notice of the fact that there just wasn't enough fried chicken to go around. Not to be outdone, she quietly pulled several of her thirteen children aside and told them to politely decline any chicken when the platter was passed. The children did as they had been instructed, and there was enough chicken for all the cousins.

When it came time for dessert—a special treat, bread pudding, Therese again made some quick calculations and decided that there wasn't enough pudding for the whole group. Just before dessert was served, she stood up and said sternly: "All of you kids that didn't care to eat my fried chicken will not get any of my dessert!" (Raising and feeding thirteen children had done wonders for Therese Delahoussaye's ingenuity.) The meal ended successfully, and those little Delahoussayes who helped save the day undoubtedly were given a special treat when the guests departed.

# Cajun MEN COOK
## DESSERTS

# DESSERTS

# MOM'S SWEET POTATO PIE

2 cups mashed cooked
  yams (canned is okay)
2 tablespoons butter
½ teaspoon salt
2 cups sugar
½ teaspoon cinnamon
¼ teaspoon cloves (ground)
½ teaspoon nutmeg (grated)

2 medium eggs, slightly
  beaten
1 cup milk
⅔ cup evaporated milk
1 teaspoon vanilla
1 plain 9 inch pie shell
2 teaspoons pecans,
  chopped (optional)

Boil yams in skin for 30 minutes. Drain, peel and mash. Beat potatoes with food processor or by hand. Add butter, sugar, salt and spices and mix. Add eggs, milk, evaporated milk, vanilla and mix. Pour onto baking dish with edges crimped high if possible. Sprinkle pecans on top. Bake in hot oven at 425°F for 10 minutes. Reduce heat to 350°F and bake 25-30 minutes or until firm around edges, but still a little soft in the middle. Center will get firm as pie cools. Try with vanilla ice cream or whipped topping.

# NUT CLUSTERS

2 cups semi-sweet
  chocolate (chips are fine)
1 15 ounce can condensed
  milk

2 cups nuts, raisins or
  cereal

Heat this mixture on top of the stove stirring frequently until chocolate is melted and mixture is thoroughly combined. Remove from heat and stir in 2 cups of nuts, raisins or cereal (such as crisped rice). Drop the mixture on wax paper until chocolate is firm.

*Can store covered up to 2 weeks at room temperature.*

## PEANUT BUTTER COOKIES

2½ cups flour
½ teaspoon salt
½ teaspoon baking soda
1 cup margarine

1 cup peanut butter
1 cup white sugar
1 cup brown sugar
2 eggs

Mix flour, salt, baking soda and set aside. Mix margarine and peanut butter. Add both kinds of sugar and mix well. Add eggs and beat well. Stir flour mixture into peanut butter mixture. Drop dough from teaspoon onto baking pan. Flatten with fork. Bake at 375°F for 10-15 minutes or until golden brown.

*4-5 servings*

**Pecans, M & M's or crunchy peanut butter can be added.**

## RANGER COOKIES

1 stick butter
¼ teaspoon salt
½ teaspoon baking powder
½ cup sugar

1 egg
1 teaspoon vanilla
3 cups flour

Cream butter and sugar together. Beat in egg and vanilla. Add pre-sifted dry ingredients. Mix well. Chill for 20 minutes. Roll out dough on floured cutting board. Cut out cookies. Put on greased cookie sheet. Bake at 350°F for 10 minutes or until edges turn light brown.

*2 dozen*

# BONNE ANNEE COOKIES

1 cup butter
2 cups sugar
5 eggs
5 cups flour
2 tablespoons baking powder

1 tablespoon baking soda
2 tablespoons salt
¼ cup milk
1 tablespoon vanilla or lemon flavor

Cream together butter and sugar. Add eggs one at a time. Sift dry ingredients and add alternately with milk and flavoring. Refrigerate 1 hour or longer. Knead dough on well floured board and cut with cookie cutter (¼ inch thick). Bake on ungreased cookie sheet 350°F for 12 to 15 minutes. Use powdered sugar icing with oil of anise flavoring.

# MARIONETTES

1 block oleo (¼ pound)
1 block butter (¼ pound)
½ cup sugar
⅓ box (+1 or 2) honey graham crackers

15½x10½ inch jelly roll pan
1 cup pecans, chopped (more if desired)

Break honey grahams in half, and then half again, and line pan with crackers. Sprinkle chopped pecans over all the grahams. Melt oleo and butter in small pan and add ½ cup sugar. Bring mixture to a boil and boil 2 minutes. Spoon over top of grahams and pecans. Bake in 325°F oven for about 18 minutes. Remove with spatula and place on waxed paper. They will harden as they cool.

*48 cookies*

**This recipe won First Place and Best of Show at cookie bake in San Francisco.**

# CAJUN CRACKER JACKS

1 stick butter
1 cup brown sugar
1 cup dark Karo syrup
1 cup sugar

1 teaspoon vanilla
2 cups Spanish peanuts, raw
4 quarts popcorn, popped

Melt butter in baking pan, and add all ingredients except popcorn, bring to a roaring boil. Remove from fire and pour over popcorn. Mix well. Bake in oven at 350°F for 30 minutes. Remove and stir a few times as mixture cools to help separate popcorn.

*10 servings*


# FATTY PATTIES

**Crust:**
1 box butter cake mix
(chocolate or yellow)
1 stick softened butter

1 teaspoon vanilla extract
2 eggs
½ cup chopped pecans

Beat and spread into 9x12 inch pan.

**Topping:**
8 ounces softened cream cheese
3 eggs

1 box powdered sugar
1 teaspoon vanilla extract

Beat until smooth. Pour over crust. Bake at 300°F for 45 minutes or until light brown.

# BANANA SPLIT CAKE

4 bananas
1 box lite cake mix, yellow
(reduced fat)
1 16 ounce can crushed
pineapple sweetened in its
own juice

1 box vanilla instant
pudding
1 large carton whipped
topping (lite)
1 small jar of cherries

Prepare cake mix according to directions and bake in a 9x13 inch pan. Let cool. Spread pineapple over cake. Slice bananas over this, covering pineapple completely. Prepare pudding according to directions and let chill until thickened, then spread over bananas. Top with cherries and whipped topping and refrigerate until ready to serve.

# STERLING'S CRUMB CAKE

2 cans pie filling (your
choice)
cinnamon and sugar
pecans

1 box cake mix (preferably
white)
1 stick melted butter

Preheat oven to 375°F. Grease a 9x13 inch pan. Pour the 2 cans of pie filling into the pan. Sprinkle cinnamon and sugar and pecans over the filling. Pour ½ of the cake mix over the filling. Pour ½ stick of melted butter over the mix. Pour the remaining cake mix in the pan with the rest of the melted butter. Layer everything. **DO NOT** mix everything together or it will not turn out! Bake for 45 minutes.

*You may serve hot or cold. Fantastic with a scoop of ice cream on top of each serving!*

# TRADITIONAL DESSERTS

Acadiana cooks, justifiably celebrated for their tasty culinary innovations, displayed remarkably little imagination in producing desserts during the first half of the twentieth century. Traditional desserts relied heavily upon the ingredients most readily available—particularly eggs, sugar, syrup, and fruit preserves. Sweet dough pies, fig cakes, syrup cakes, popcorn balls, pralines, and cobblers were the most common baked treats. Multilayered cakes were generally made for special occasions, while homemade ice cream was a Sunday treat in summertime.

## FIG POUND CAKE

1 cup sugar
1 block butter
2-3 eggs
2½ cups flour
1 teaspoon cinnamon
1 teaspoon nutmeg
1 cup buttermilk

1 pint fig preserves
1 cup pecans, chopped
  (optional)
1 teaspoon soda
½ cup shredded coconut
  (optional)

Stir together sugar, butter and eggs; add cinnamon, nutmeg, and soda. Measure milk and add vinegar to milk. When milk thickens, pour with rest of ingredients. Stir in flour until well blended. Stir in figs and pecans. Bake in a tube pan greased and floured. Cook for 1 hour at 350°F or 375°F or until done.

*10-14 servings*

**Good as a coffee cake, too. Very rich. Good holiday cake.**

**Better when 2 days old.**

# CARROT CAKE

2 cups sugar
4 eggs
1½ cups cooking oil
2 teaspoons soda

1 teaspoon salt
3 teaspoons cinnamon
3 cups shredded carrots
2 cups flour

Mix sugar, eggs, and oil. Add flour, soda, salt and cinnamon. Mix well; add carrots and mix real good. Bake in 4 layers at 325°F for 20 to 30 minutes. Cool and frost.

**Frosting:**
¼ pound oleo
3 cups pecans
2 teaspoons vanilla

1 pound box powdered sugar
1 16 ounce package cream cheese

Add all ingredients together and mix real well. Add to cool cake layers and top.

*1 large cake (4 layers)*

**The cooking time may be different because all ovens do not cook the same.**

# MANDARIN ORANGE CAKE

1 box yellow butter cake mix
½ cup vegetable oil

4 eggs
1 11 ounce can mandarin oranges

Mix cake mix, oil and eggs. Add oranges, including juice. Divide batter into three 8 inch greased and floured cake pans. Bake at 350°F for 18-20 minutes.

**Filling and Icing:**
1 3 ounce box instant vanilla pudding
1 20 ounce can crushed pineapple (including juice)

1 8 ounce container non-dairy whipped topping

Mix pudding and pineapple (including juice). Add non-dairy whipped topping and mix well. Ice layers and cake after layers have cooled completely. Chill in refrigerator before serving.

## FRUIT AND CREAM CHEESE CAKE

3 cups all purpose flour
2 cups sugar
1 teaspoon baking powder
1 teaspoon salt
1 teaspoon ground
 cinnamon
3 eggs, beaten

1 cup vegetable oil
1½ teaspoons vanilla
 extract
1 8 ounce can crushed
 pineapple, undrained
1 cup chopped pecans
2 cups chopped bananas

Combine first 3 ingredients in a large mixing bowl, add eggs and oil, stirring until dry ingredients are moistened. Do not beat. Stir in vanilla, pineapple, 1 cup pecans and bananas. Spoon batter into 3 greased and floured 9 inch round cake pans. Bake at 350°F for 25 to 30 minutes or until a wooden toothpick inserted in center comes out clean. Cool in pans for 10 minutes. Remove from pans and cool completely.

**Cream Cheese Frosting:**
1 8 ounce package cream
 cheese, softened
½ cup butter or margarine,
 softened

1 16 ounce package
 powdered sugar, sifted
1 teaspoon vanilla extract
½ cup chopped pecans

Combine cream cheese and butter, beating until smooth. Add powdered sugar and vanilla, beat until light and fluffy. Spread frosting between layers of cake and on top and sides of cake. Sprinkle ½ cup chopped pecans on top.

## EARTHQUAKE CAKE

1 cup chopped pecans
1 cup coconut
1 box German chocolate
 cake mix

1 pound powdered sugar
1 stick butter
1 8 ounce package cream
 cheese

Spray bottom of 9x13 inch cake pan with non-stick spray. Sprinkle pecans and coconut on bottom of pan. Mix cake mix as directed on box. Pour in pan. Soften cream cheese and butter. Mix in powdered sugar. Drop in small amounts on top of cake mix. Bake approximately 55 minutes in 350°F oven.

## PIÑA COLADA POUND CAKE

2 sticks butter
½ cup butter flavored
   shortening
3 cups sugar
5 eggs
1 teaspoon rum extract

1 teaspoon coconut extract
1 cup milk
3 cups flour
½ teaspoon baking powder
½ teaspoon salt

Blend butter and shortening well. Gradually add sugar. Then add eggs one at a time beating one (1) minute after each. Add extracts. Mix dry ingredients together in a separate bowl. Add dry ingredients to the mixture alternately with milk, starting and ending with flour mixture. Pour into either a tube pan or a bundt pan. Bake at 325°F for 1 hour and 15 minutes.

**Glaze:**
1 cup sugar
½ cup water

1 teaspoon almond extract

Stir sugar and water until mixture comes to a boil. Cool and add almond extract. Pour entire glaze over cake.

## CREOLE HONEY CAKE

2 sticks butter
1 cup honey
4 eggs, beaten
1½ teaspoons lemon juice
3 cups flour
2¼ tablespoons baking
   powder

½ teaspoon salt
¾ cup toasted, chopped
   pecans
1 cup fruit (figs, peaches, or
   blackberries)

Melt butter with honey. Add eggs and lemon juice. Mix well and slowly add pre-mixed flour, baking powder and salt. Add chopped fruit and pecans to the batter. The batter will be stiff. Pour into greased, floured baking pans and bake at 350°F for 30 minutes or until cake tests done. (If broom straw stuck into center comes out clean, it is done).

*8 servings*

# TURTLE CAKE

1 box German chocolate
  cake mix with pudding in
  it
1 pound caramels
1 can sweetened condensed
  milk

1 stick margarine
6 ounces chocolate chips
1 cup pecan pieces (or more
  if desired)

Mix the cake according to directions. Pour ½ of cake batter into greased and floured 9x13 inch pan. Bake for 15 minutes at 350°F. While baking, melt caramels and margarine over low heat. Gradually add condensed milk, stirring until absorbed. After 15 minutes baking time, spread the caramel mix over the cake then add the remaining ½ of the batter evenly over that. Sprinkle this with the chocolate chips and pecans. Bake at 350°F for 25 to 30 minutes.

# CHOCOLATE REFRIGERATOR CAKE

20 Lady Fingers
½ pound sweet cooking
  chocolate*
3 eggs, separated
1 teaspoon vanilla

1 cup whipping cream,
  divided
*½ cup sugar (use if
  chocolate is semisweet)

Line straight sided loaf pan, 11x4x2½ inch with waxed paper, leaving an overhang. Separate Lady Fingers. Place 8 halves in a row in bottom of pan. Melt chocolate with sugar over hot water; remove from heat. Add egg yolks, one at a time, beating vigorously after each. Beat egg whites stiff; fold in. Spread ¼ chocolate mixture on Lady Fingers in pan. Add another row of Lady Finger halves. Repeat until there are 4 layers of chocolate. Top with remaining Lady Fingers. Chill several hours or overnight. Lift cake from pan with wax paper overhang. Remove wax paper. Place on serving dish. Whip remaining cream. Use to frost sides of loaf. (Optional: Add chopped pecans to chocolate mixture).

*Makes 8-10 servings*

**No cooking! Delicious!**

# COCONUT DELUXE POUND CAKE

**Cake:**

| | |
|---|---|
| **2 sticks oleo** | **1 teaspoon rum extract** |
| **½ cup shortening** | **3 cups flour** |
| **3 cups sugar** | **½ teaspoon baking powder** |
| **5 large eggs** | **⅓ teaspoon salt** |
| **1 teaspoon coconut extract** | **1 cup milk** |

Blend oleo and shortening. Add sugar. Blend in eggs, one at a time. Beat one minute after adding each egg. Separately, mix flour, baking powder, and salt. Add flour mix to egg and sugar mix blending in with milk. Bake at 350°F for approximately 1½ hours. Test with broom straw. When straw comes out clean after puncturing cake, the cake is done. While cake is baking, make glaze. When cake is cooled and placed on plate, poke holes in it with a fork and pour glaze over cake

Glaze: Bring 1 cup sugar and ½ cup water to a boil. Take it off of burner immediately. Cool, then add 1 teaspoon almond extract.

# THE KING CAKE TRADITION

South Louisiana's Mardi Gras tradition is known throughout the world, but the sharing of frosted cakes, an important feature of the Louisiana Mardi Gras season, is little known outside the Pelican State.

The Mardi Gras season actually begins on January 6, the Feast of the Epiphany (Twelfth Night). This feast day commemorates the presentation of gifts to the Christ child by the Magi. The season continues through Shrove Tuesday (Mardi Gras), the day before Ash Wednesday. Mardi Gras day is the final celebration before Christians begin the Lenten season.

King cakes were first introduced into Louisiana's Mardi Gras traditions by the Twelfth Night Revelers, a New Orleans party organization, during the 1870 celebration. A king cake with a "golden" bean baked into it was sliced and distributed among the ladies of the court. The lady whose slice contained the bean was crowned the queen of the festival. Most king cakes now contain plastic babies, and tradition dictates that the person receiving the slice with the baby is obligated to buy the next cake.

King cakes are common in school rooms, business offices, and homes during Louisiana's Mardi Gras season. In recent years some bakers have altered the sweet dough cake by including fruit or cream cheese fillings.

## KING CAKE

**Dough:**

5-6 cups all purpose flour
2 packages yeast
⅔ cup warm water (105°F-115°F)
1 cup warm milk (105°F-115°F)
½ cup sugar
1½ teaspoon salt
½ teaspoon freshly grated nutmeg
¼ cup butter or margarine
2 eggs
cooking oil

**Filling and Glaze:**
1 cup packed brown sugar
⅔ cup chopped pecans
½ cup All Purpose flour
½ cup raisins

2 tablespoons ground
   cinnamon
½ cup butter or margarine
   (melted)
1 cup confectioners' sugar

Scald milk, remove from heat and put butter in milk to soften - allow to cool. Sprinkle yeast over warm water to which a tablespoon of sugar has been added. Rinse a large mixing bowl under very warm water and dry. When yeast mixture is bubbling pour into large bowl and add milk testing that it has cooled and is slightly warm to skin of arm. Add 2 eggs and whisk until frothy. Add one or two cups of flour, sugar, salt and nutmeg. Beat well until all ingredients are blended and elastic. Add another cup of flour and beat. When mixture becomes thick and leaves sides of bowl, turn out onto floured board or counter top. Knead dough and add remaining flour sprinkling on surface used for kneading. Knead until smooth - approximately 10 minutes. Grease another large bowl with cooking oil. Put dough into bowl then turn over dough so oiled surface is up. Cover with damp kitchen towel or plastic wrap. Place in warm place until double in size - about 1-2 hours. When risen, punch down, divide dough in half or in four. Roll dough into rectangles. Sprinkle rectangles with filling. Roll up like jelly roll beginning at wide side. Seal ends well. Form into ovals on greased 4x9 inch cake pans or 2 large cookie sheets. With scissors, make cuts ⅓ of the way through the ring at 1 inch intervals. Let rise. Bake 30 minutes at 375°F. Frost while warm with 1 cup confectioners' sugar blended with 1 or 2 tablespoons of water. For filling mix all dry ingredients except confectioners' sugar. Pour melted butter over this and mix until crumbly. Decorate with sugar dyed purple, green and gold with food coloring or just decorate cakes with pecans and cherries. A plastic doll or three dried beans may be put into filling before rolling up or they may be pushed into dough from bottom after baking. The person getting the doll has the next King Cake party or the children getting the three beans are the Three Wise Men.

# PIE CRUST

1⅓ cups plain flour
1 teaspoon salt

⅓ cup cooking oil
3 tablespoons whole milk

Measure oil into cup and add milk. Pour into flour and salt mixture. Roll out mixture between 2 sheets of waxed paper. Peel off top sheet of waxed paper and invert pie plate on crust. Flip over, peel off paper and fit crust into pie pan. Bake at 450°F for 12 minutes.

*1 pie crust*

# CHOCOLATE SIN

1 stick soft margarine
1 cup flour
½ cup finely chopped
 pecans
8 ounces cream cheese
1 cup powdered sugar

1 large size whipped
 topping
2 packages instant
 chocolate pudding
3 cups milk

Mix margarine, flour and most of the pecans and pat into a 9x13 inch Pyrex pan. Bake for 15 minutes and cool. Mix cream cheese, sugar and 1 cup of topping. Spread this carefully over the first layer in the pan. Mix the milk into the pudding and beat for 2 minutes. Spread this over second layer. Spread the remaining topping on top and sprinkle with remaining chopped pecans. Refrigerate. When ready to serve, cut into squares and stand aside!

# JUNIOR'S PECAN PIE

1 cup dark brown sugar
1 cup light brown sugar
⅓ cup melted butter (=5.28
 tablespoons)
⅓ teaspoon salt

1 teaspoon vanilla extract
3 eggs, slightly beaten
1 9 inch deep dish pie shell
1 heaping cup pecan halves

Preheat oven to 350°F. In a large mixing bowl, combine brown sugar, corn syrup, melted butter, salt, and vanilla; stir well. Add beaten eggs and beat the mixture with an electric mixer for 2 to 3 minutes. Pour the mixture into pie shell. Sprinkle the pecan halves evenly over the top. Bake at 350°F for 45 minutes, or until firm. Let the pie cool before cutting and serving.

# HEAVENLY PECAN PIE

**Pie Crust:**

1 cup flour
½ teaspoon salt

⅓ cup shortening
3 tablespoons ice water

Mix flour and salt together. Cut in shortening. Add cold water and mix. Roll out dough on floured board to fit bottom and sides of pie pan.

**Filling:**

3 eggs, well beaten
½ cup white sugar
1 cup light corn syrup

2 tablespoons melted butter
1 teaspoon vanilla
1 cup pecans

Pour all ingredients into unbaked pie crust. Bake 15 minutes at 400°F, then bake another 30 minutes at 325°F.

# STRAWBERRY DELIGHT

1 3 ounce package
  strawberry flavored
  gelatin
1¼ cup boiling water
1 10 ounce package sliced
  frozen strawberries

1 tablespoon sugar
pinch of salt
1 10 inch angel food cake
  (torn into pieces)
½ pint whipping cream
small jar of cherries

Dissolve gelatin in 1¼ cups boiling water. Stir in thawed strawberries, sugar and salt. Cool until it begins to thicken and then put in refrigerator. Fold in cream, whipped. Cover bottom of pan or casserole with half the torn angel food cake. Pour half the strawberry and cream mixture over cake. Put another layer of rest of angel food cake and then pour over remaining strawberry and cream mixture. Refrigerate 4 to 5 hours before serving. Cut into squares and put cherry on top of each square to serve.

*8 servings*

**May be made the day before.**

# HOMEMADE ICE CREAM AT PA-PA'S

My fondest childhood memories center on the family gatherings held each Sunday at my grandfather's house. Each Sunday after church, my mother and father and their four screaming savages joined my aunt, her husband, and their ten screaming banshees in a full-scale invasion of my grandfather's rural residence.

Despite the pre-pubescent tumult swirling around him, my grandfather was clearly in his element. Pa-Pa lived for these gatherings. He always managed to find time for each of his grandchildren. He also somehow managed to feed all of us. And the pièce de resistance at each summer meal was homemade ice cream. All of the kids took turns turning the crank on Pa-Pa's ancient, but incredibly sturdy freezer until after what seemed hours, thc adults pronounced the ice cream "done." Put away until after the meal, that homemade ice cream was the best antidote against the heat and humidity in those now distant pre-air conditioning days.

## OLD FASHIONED ICE CREAM

| | |
|---|---|
| 2 tablespoons vanilla<br>flavoring | 1¾ cups sugar<br>6 teaspoons corn starch |
| 2 quarts milk | 1 large can evaporated milk |
| 6 eggs | |

Beat eggs and add sugar, a little at a time, and mix well. Add corn starch slowly and mix well. Pour milk in pot and add evaporated milk. Stir well. When milk starts to boil, add mixture and cook on low heat. Stir for 15 minutes as mixture cooks. Add vanilla and stir. Put into ice cream freezer and freeze.

# A "DIFFERENT" BREAD PUDDING

½ cup (bit less than 1 stick) unsalted butter, softened
10 or more 1 inch French bread slices
4 eggs

¾ cup sugar, plus 2 tablespoons for topping
4 cups low-fat milk
2 teaspoons vanilla extract
nutmeg (regular or freshly grated)

Preheat oven to 350°F. Turn down to 325°F when putting pudding in to cook. Grease ovenproof casserole with butter. Spread remainder of the butter on one side of bread slices and place them in a single layer on bottom of casserole, buttered side down. Beat eggs and ¾ cup sugar in large bowl. Pour in milk, stirring. Add vanilla extract and stir. Add few good shakes of nutmeg. Pour mixture carefully through strainer over bread in casserole. The bread will float to the top. Sprinkle 2 tablespoons (or more) of sugar on top of slices. Put casserole in larger ovenproof pan and surround with enough boiling water to come ½ inch up sides of casserole. Put pan in center of oven and reduce heat to 325°F. Bake 45 minutes or bake a few minutes less, and turn broiler on for a minute or two to toast the top to a golden brown.

*This pudding is very light because it calls for low-fat milk instead of cream and whole milk.*

**During "peach season", mash a few ripe ones with bit of sugar and lemon juice — makes a delicious "sauce" over individual servings.**

# PEACH COBBLER

**Crust: Batter**

½ cup flour
¾ cup sugar
½ teaspoon baking powder

2 tablespoons butter, melted
1 large egg, beaten slightly

Combine all batter ingredients.

**Filling:**

5 cups sliced peaches, fresh
½ cup sugar
4 tablespoons flour
1½ teaspoons lemon juice

½ teaspoon vanilla
¼ teaspoon almond extract
¾ teaspoon cinnamon
2 tablespoons butter

Mix the peaches lightly with sugar, flour, lemon juice, extract and cinnamon. Place in a greased pan. Cover with crust batter and chunks of butter. Bake in oven at 350°F for 30 minutes or until batter is light brown and filling is set.

*8 servings*

# WHOLE WHEAT MUFFINS

1 cup sifted flour
3 teaspoons baking powder
1 teaspoon salt
2 tablespoons sugar

1 cup whole wheat flour
1 egg
3 tablespoons melted butter
1 cup milk

Sift flour, baking powder, salt and sugar. Add whole wheat flour and mix together. Beat egg in separate bowl. Add butter and milk. Add liquid ingredients. Stir slowly to barely moisten dry ingredients. Do not beat. Preheat oven to 425°F. Fill greased muffin tins ¾ full. Bake at 425°F for 20-25 minutes.

*20-25 muffins*

# BANANAS FARLEY

½ cup butter or margarine
1 cup light-brown sugar,
  firmly packed
8 ripe bananas, peeled and
  split lengthwise

¼ teaspoon cinnamon
1 cup white rum
½ cup banana liqueur
  (Crème de Banana)
vanilla ice cream

Melt butter and brown sugar in flat chafing dish or large, attractive skillet. Arrange bananas in a single layer, and sauté, turning once, until tender - about 5 minutes. Sprinkle with cinnamon; pour in rum and banana liqueur. Ignite with match; remove from heat, and baste bananas until flame burns out. Serve at once with vanilla ice cream.

*8 servings*

# BANANAS FOSTER

2 ripe bananas, peeled,
  sliced lengthwise
1 teaspoon lemon juice,
  fresh
¼ cup brown sugar
¼ cup white rum

2 tablespoons butter
⅛ teaspoon cinnamon
2 tablespoons banana
  liqueur
1 pint vanilla ice cream

Brush banana slices with lemon juice. Melt sugar and butter in flat chafing dish or 10 inch skillet. Add bananas and sauté until tender. Sprinkle with cinnamon. Remove from heat. Add liqueur and rum. Immediately ignite and baste bananas with warm liquid until flame burns out. Divide sauce and bananas over 4 servings of ice cream.

*4 servings*

**This is a classy end to a perfect Cajun/Creole feast.**

# PAW

As a professional cook, I work with a variety of fish. I was six years old when I cleaned my first fish under the watchful eye of my grandfather, Robert Erskine Rosser, whom I called "Paw". That day at Henderson, I caught a four-inch sacalait and Paw insisted that we keep it. He showed me how to cut and scale the sacalait, and then we fried the fish. I was so proud when he announced that I had taken care of this fish myself.

Paw is gone now, but I can't cut fish without thinking of the lazy days we spent on his boat Trouble. His favorite food was stuffed flounder. So Paw, I created this low-fat, low-sodium recipe for you. Submitted by Chef Randall Rosser. (See recipe on page 216).

# CELEBRITIES' RECIPES

## MEN COOK

## STUFFED FLOUNDER ERSKINE

1 cup raw shrimp, diced
2 tablespoons soy sauce

2 tablespoons lime juice

Combine and set aside.

1 yellow onion, diced
1 red pepper, diced
2 garlic cloves, minced

1 tablespoon butter
salt, pepper and hot sauce
  to taste

Sauté in butter for 3 minutes.

½ cup white wine

shrimp mixture

Add and remove from heat. Then add:

1 cup cooked cold rice

4 boneless, skinless
  flounder fillets (about 7"
  long and 3" wide - lay on
  surface)

With skin-side up, divide mixture into 4 and place a portion in the center of the fish. Fold sides over stuffing. Turn fish over onto a non-stick sheet pan. Sprinkle with paprika and bake at 325° for 30 minutes.

*4 servings*

**Low-fat, low-sodium recipe.**

*Randall Rosser, C.C.*

# BLUE RIBBON CHEFS OF CAJUN COUNTRY

Close family ties are common in Cajun society. Indeed, cousins four or five times removed are still considered close kin. In Cajun country, social gatherings involved family and close friends. These events usually had two major elements: music and food, both of which remain an integral part of Cajuns' *joie de vivre.*

In the days of *boucheries,* when Cajun families gathered to butcher a hog or a steer, children (especially the boys) were called upon to help with the butchering and the meat preparation. Children were given increasingly difficult tasks until they were deemed sufficiently knowledgeable and skillful to take over. As a result, children naturally learned cooking skills. These skills were utilized on frequent trips to hunting and fishing camps, where female members of the families were rarely invited. "Your boy sure knows how to cook a gumbo" were sweet words to any father's ears. Since men usually cooked at the camps, it is hardly surprising that most Cajun chefs are men. This is rapidly changing today, however, as increasing numbers of young women become fine Cajun chefs.

When interviewed, these fine chefs usually credit relatives with specific recipes. Cajuns often associate relatives with specific dishes, such as "It was a family tradition that Aunt Mary or Uncle Joseph would always cook so-and-so at wedding celebrations." Names of the recipes' originators, however, are frequently forgotten over time, and chefs' names consequently become associated with the dishes.

The Beaver Club is proud to present a collection of prize-winning recipes from Acadiana's outstanding chefs. Some of the recipes are originals, but most have been handed down from past generations. These recipes have been refined and honed by the expertise, skill, and special secrets of the contributing chefs, who now share these culinary treasures, with one stipulation— "ENJOY!"

*(For more information regarding these Ambassadors of Cajun Country and the fine restaurants they represent, contact the Lafayette Convention and Visitors Commission at 1-800-346-1958.)*

# STUFFED VEAL ROAST

1 2-3 pound veal roast
1 cup wild rice, uncooked
1 red bell pepper, chopped
½ cup mushrooms, chopped
1 yellow bell pepper,
  chopped

2 tablespoons garlic,
  chopped
1 medium onion, minced
¼ cup white wine vinegar

**Sauce:**
1 quart veal stock
½ cup white roux
1 cup Maderia wine

season to taste
2 sprigs rosemary

With sharp knife, slit roast down middle, leave large pocket. Mix next nine ingredients and fill pocket of roast. Tie roast with string to secure stuffing. Season to taste and bake at 350°F for 45 minutes in large roasting pan. In saucepan, combine first four ingredients of sauce. Thicken with white roux. When roast is cooked, slice into rounds and serve with sauce.

*10 servings*

*Wayne Jean, Chef*
*Charley G's Restaurant*
*Lafayette, LA*

*One of the things that makes Cajun cooking so special is the fact that it was developed using only the ingredients which Cajuns could grow, hunt or catch themselves. Cajuns make for wonderful farmers and agriculture is still a mainstay of the economy of South Louisiana...with Crowley, Louisiana positioning themselves as the Rice Capital of the World. This has caused a little bit of worry for one Beaver Club member:*

> *"As I drove through our beautiful Cajun countryside the other day, I noticed the thousands of acres of rice. I was so proud. But then I started to worry...just how much gravy was it going to take to cover all that rice!"*

*He really shouldn't worry—any Cajun will tell you that rice is a mainstay of any lunch or dinner and not just with gravy. You need it for your gumbo, your étouffée, your red beans...*

# DON'S STUFFED CRABS

1 pound white crabmeat
½ cup bell pepper, chopped
1 pound claw meat
2 cloves garlic minced
4 stale hamburger buns (or 6 slices stale white bread)
1 cup evaporated milk
½ teaspoon Worcestershire sauce
¼ pound oleo (or ½ cup vegetable oil)

1 cup chopped onions
3 large eggs
½ cup chopped celery
¼ cup chopped green onion tops
salt, black pepper and cayenne red pepper to taste
¼ cup chopped parsley

Sauté onions, celery, garlic and chopped bell pepper in a heavy pot in the oleo or oil on medium heat until wilted, about 2 minutes. Add Worcestershire sauce, crabmeat and season to taste with salt, red pepper and black pepper. Cook over medium heat about 15 minutes, stirring constantly. Add onion tops and parsley. Then add buns which have been soaked in the milk and whisked eggs. Mix well; stuff crab shells with mixture. Use about 12 artificial crab shells. Sprinkle tops of stuffed crabs with bread crumbs and bake in oven at 375°F for 10 minutes or until well browned.

*6 servings*

**Don's Seafood and Steakhouse is an original landmark restaurant in Lafayette having been established in 1934. Ownership remains in the Landry family which carries on a proud tradition. Fresh seafood is served daily. Prepared with a Cajun/Continental flair, the end product yields food dishes applauded by both local and world wide clientele.**

*Rocky Landry, Owner, Chef*
*Don's Seafood and Steakhouse*
*Lafayette, LA*

# CRABMEAT À LA LANDRY

1 cup onions, chopped fine
¼ pound butter or oleo
⅓ cup celery, chopped fine
2 cups cornflakes
⅛ teaspoon sage
1 13 ounce can evaporated
milk
⅛ teaspoon thyme

⅛ teaspoon nutmeg
1 pound lump crabmeat
⅛ teaspoon oregano
1 cup butter crackers,
crumbled
⅛ teaspoon marjoram
1 tablespoon flour

Sauté onions and celery in oleo or butter until onions are wilted.
Add crabmeat, sage, thyme, nutmeg, oregano, marjoram, evaporated milk and flour. Toast the cornflakes in the oven at 325°F until crisp; crumble; then blend well into crabmeat mix. Put into individual ramekins or casseroles. Sprinkle with crumbled crackers. Add a pat of butter on top of each ramekin and bake for 20 minutes at 375°F.

*6 servings*

***Don's Seafood and Steakhouse is a family run business since 1934. It is noted for consistency in flavor and high quality of food served. Rocky Landry, proudly carries on this tradition at one of Lafayette's premier restaurants.***

*Rocky Landry, Owner, Chef*
*Don's Seafood and Steakhouse*
*Lafayette, LA*

# BROCCOLI SOUP, CHASTANT

1 medium head of broccoli, chopped fine
¼ teaspoon white pepper
¼ teaspoon red pepper
1 large onion, chopped fine
1 pint Half-n-Half cream
½ large bell pepper, chopped fine

4 tablespoons flour
3 tablespoons olive oil
1 tablespoon chicken base
1 pint water (or 2 chicken bouillon cubes or 2 cups of chicken stock)

On medium fire heat olive oil in a skillet and then add flour; stir 5 minutes until blond roux is creamy. Set aside. In a 6 quart pot add water and boil; add broccoli, and other vegetables; boil on medium heat covered, until tender. Remove water add hot chicken stock, seasonings and roux. Simmer 10 minutes until well blended. Add cream and stir until well blended; simmer 5 minutes. Adjust salt and other seasonings. Serve hot.

*6 servings*

**This rich soup is usually served along with the salad as a first course. Entrée. Hot buttered fresh bread is ideal with this menu combination.**

*Mike Chastant, Chef*
*Oyster Reef Restaurant*
*Lafayette, LA*

## CARIBBEAN LIME SOUFFLÉ

2 envelopes unflavored
  gelatin
4 drops or more of green
  food coloring
1½ cup whole milk
4 eggs, separated

1 teaspoon cream of tartar
¼ cup sugar
¾ cup whipping cream
1 6¼ ounce can or package
  frozen limeade
  concentrate

Sprinkle gelatin over milk in a small saucepan; let it stand 5 minutes to soften. Cover over low heat until gelatin dissolves, about 10 minutes; stir to keep milk from sticking; set aside. In a 4 quart bowl, beat egg yolks and sugar together. Add limeade concentrate and food coloring. Add gelatin and milk mix; chill until mixture is thick enough to mound from a spoon. In a 1 quart bowl beat egg whites with cream of tartar until stiff, fold both into gelatin mix; turn into a 5 cup soufflé dish which has been extended with a 2 inch foil collar. Chill until set; remove collar; garnish with fruit and serve, chilled.

*8 servings*

**This is a light, delightful dessert, ideal for ending a full course meal.**

*Marco Arquelles, Chef*
*City Club of Lafayette*
*Lafayette, LA*

## CHUCK WAGON STEW

1½ pound round steak
4 medium potatoes, diced
1 tablespoon shortening
2 cups sliced carrots
2 tablespoons flour
2 cups sliced apples
4 cups beef broth or
  consommé, boiling

12 pearl or small onions,
  whole
2 bay leaves
salt and pepper to taste
½ tablespoon browning and
  seasoning sauce (optional)

Cut steak in ¾x4 inch strips and roll in flour; melt shortening in a 4 quart pot on medium heat for 5 minutes; fry and brown steak; add boiling beef stock and seasonings; simmer, covered, for two hours; add remaining ingredients and low simmer for 1½ hours longer. Serve over steaming rice.

*4 servings*

**This is a typical Cajun all-in-one noon rice and gravy dish. Lima beans, corn macque choux, cabbage salad, corn bread and tea would complete this meal.**

*Marco Arquelles, Chef*
*City Club of Lafayette*
*Lafayette, LA*

## HOT CRAWFISH SPINACH SALAD

½ cup vegetable oil
1 12 ounce bunch fresh
 spinach
1 small onion, finely
 chopped
2 cloves garlic, finely
 chopped

1 medium tomato, diced
¼ rice wine vinegar
½ cup mushrooms, sliced
6 ounces crawfish tails
½ lemon, sliced thin
⅛ teaspoon cayenne pepper

Heat oil in small saucepan over medium heat; when oil is hot, add onion and garlic; sauté for 2 minutes until tender. Whisk in mustard, vinegar, and cayenne. Season to taste with salt and black pepper. Fold in crawfish. Cook to warm through. Break spinach into bite size pieces and place in a bowl. Pour crawfish dressing over spinach, toss to coat. Portion on 2 salad plates. Garnish with tomato, lemon and mushrooms.

*4 servings*

**This tasty salad dish would compliment any seafood menu.**

*Blue Ribbon Chef of Cajun Bayou Country -
Chef Marty Cosgrove of Paul Prudhomme's*

*Famous for their incredible cuisine and their unusual edibles (after all, who else would have ever thought to try crawfish— those "mudbugs" Cajuns can't get enough of!) Cajuns are often kidded that they will eat anything. While this is meant as a good natured insult, Cajuns take it as a compliment as is evident by this story passed on by one Beaver Club member:*

> *"A tourist noted that the new Cajun Zoo he went to on his visit to Acadiana was unlike any other zoo he'd ever been to. They had all the usual animals and on each cage there was a sign that showed the zoological name of the animal followed by the common name. This was then followed by a recipe on how to prepare the animal for consumption."*

*Cajuns know that if they find a way to cook it, the whole world will soon want to eat it!!*

# MIKE'S CRAWFISH PASTA

2 pounds crawfish tails
2 tablespoons flour
1 12 ounce package
   fettuccine pasta
4 tablespoons olive oil
2 cups water
1 bell pepper, chopped fine

1½ teaspoon red pepper
4 stalks celery, chopped
   fine
1 tablespoon salt
1 bunch green onion tops,
   chopped fine
¼ cup butter

In a 1 quart skillet, on medium fire, heat 2 tablespoons of olive oil. Add flour and stir until flour turns into a tan colored roux. Set aside. Prepare pasta according to directions on package adding 2 tablespoons of olive oil to the finish product; set aside. Melt butter in a 6 quart pot; add bell pepper and celery and then cook about 10 minutes on medium heat until tender. Add crawfish, 2 cups of boiling water and roux. Simmer about 15 minutes until thickens; add seasonings and onion tops and serve warm, on top of pasta.

*8 servings*

**This is one of Mike's specialties and is a complete menu if served with a wop salad and toasted garlic French bread.**

*Mike Chastant, Chef*
*Oyster Reef Restaurant*
*Lafayette, LA*

# SHOCKLEY'S CRAWFISH DIP

2 tablespoons onions, minced
1 tablespoon Vermouth
2 tablespoons parsley, minced
½ teaspoon black pepper
2 tablespoons green onions, chopped fine
½ teaspoon red pepper
1 teaspoon granulated garlic

2 tablespoons butter
1 10¾ ounce can Cream of Mushroom soup
1 teaspoon Cajun blended season mix
1 12 ounce package cream cheese
1 12 ounce pack crawfish meat

Sauté onion, green onion, and parsley in butter on medium heat until soft. Add Vermouth and mushroom soup; bring to a boil and then add cheese and melt; stir in crawfish meat; add seasonings, and reduce heat to simmer; about 2 minutes. Keep warm in a chafing dish during serving.

*This popular hors d'oeuvres is always requested as an entrée when Chef Shockley caters at the Washington, D.C. annual Mardi Gras Ball.*

*1 quart*

*Britt Shockley, Chef*
*Broussard Catering*
*Lafayette, LA*

# MARDI GRAS CHICKEN/CRAWFISH

2 tablespoons butter
½ cup green bell pepper, chopped fine
2 quarts heavy cream
3½ cups canned or fresh whole kernel corn
⅓ cup green bell pepper, chopped fine
1½ teaspoons all season mix
1⅓ tablespoon Italian parsley (flat leaf)
¾ cup tasso, diced julienne
1½ cups raw crawfish or shrimp
1½ cup baked chicken meat
½ cup green onion, chopped
2⅔ tablespoons fresh Parmesan cheese, chopped fine

Melt butter in a large skillet; add corn and heavy cream; cook on medium heat until cream coats a wooden spoon, about 20 minutes. Add tasso and bell peppers and cook for 2 minutes; add seasonings and stir for 1 minute; add chicken and crawfish and cook for 3 minutes or until sauce thickens again. Add green onions, parsley and Parmesan cheese. Serve over angel hair pasta.

*8 servings*

***This is an excellent way to use leftover baked fowl such as chicken, turkey or duck. With its festive Mardi Gras colors it is ideal for a covered dish party!***

*Roy Lyons, Owner, Chef*
*Café Acadie*
*Crowley, LA*

# OYSTER ALINE

**3 dozen large oysters, clean
reserve shells**

Clean and retain oyster juice, meat and shells.

**Roasted Pepper Stuffing:**

**2 large red bell peppers**
**1 cup oyster liquid, from
  oysters**
**2½ pounds of tasso or sugar
  cured ham, diced**
**1 teaspoon Cajun blended
  seasonings**

**1 cup butter**
**1½ cup onion, minced**
**1 teaspoon red pepper**
**1 tablespoon garlic, minced**
**1 teaspoon black pepper**
**1½ cup bread crumbs, plain**
**1 teaspoon salt**

Mix Cajun blended seasonings, salt, red and black pepper together in a small bowl; set aside. Roast, skin, and finely chop red peppers. Set aside. (To roast, bake uncovered on a cookie sheet at 375°F for about 20 minutes). In a skillet sauté onion, and garlic in butter until limp, about 5 minutes on medium heat; fold in tasso and cook for 5 minutes on medium heat. Because of the variance of the tasso or ham, you must now taste the mixture and adjust the seasonings by adding the seasoning blend one teaspoon at a time to prevent over seasoning; set final product aside.

**Crab and Shrimp Stuffing:**

**4 tablespoons butter**
**¾ cup oyster juice from
  oysters**
**1 cup onions, minced**
**½ cup mushrooms, minced**
**¾ teaspoon cayenne red
  pepper**
**2 pounds of fresh 90/110
  count small shrimp,
  peeled**

**¾ teaspoon salt**
**¾ teaspoon black pepper**
**1 pound of white crabmeat**
**¾ teaspoon Cajun blended
  seasonings**
**½ cup Vermouth**
**1¼ pint heavy cream**
**1¼ cup bread crumbs,
  plain, or soft French
  bread**

Mix all dry seasonings in a small bowl; set aside. Sauté onions and mushrooms in butter until tender. Add shrimp, cream, Vermouth and oyster liquor; cook on low fire until shrimp are cooked, about 10 minutes. Add crabmeat, ½ of seasonings, and bread crumbs, only enough to tighten. (Not too dry). Soft French bread, added a little at a time, can be substituted for bread crumbs.

Add amounts of remaining seasonings according to taste test; fill ½ of oyster barquette shell with crab/shrimp mix and the other half with the red pepper mix. Place on a cookie sheet or in a baking pan and bake at 400°F for 20 minutes. Serve hot.

*The unique blend of bell pepper and tasso with shrimp and crabmeat brings out the full bouquet of flavor of the oyster. Tasso is a lean pork Cajun ham. This dish is named after Britt's Maternal Grandmother, 82 year old Aline Butcher.*

**Serve with creamed potatoes flavored with garlic butter, petit pois, French bread and wine.**

*Britt Shockley*
*Broussard Catering*
*Lafayette, LA*

## ITALIAN BALSAMIC VINAIGRETTE

**2¼ cups Balsamic vinegar**
**1 teaspoon marjoram leaves, dry**
**2½ teaspoons salt**
**1 tablespoon garlic, minced**
**1 teaspoon fennel seed,**
**1 teaspoon oregano, crushed**

**½ teaspoon ground basil leaves**
**1 ounce parsley, minced**
**½ teaspoon black pepper**
**1 teaspoon dry thyme leaves**
**2¼ cups olive oil**

Mix seasonings, herbs and mustard together; whisk in olive oil in thin stream until all is incorporated. Stir into a clean container with a tight lid. Cover and refrigerate. Shake prior to serving.

*This is one of the best vinaigrettes I have used thus far. It stores well and brings salad ingredients to life.*

**Rub a slice of French bread garlic toast on inner surface of salad bowl. Leave in until after tossing then remove.**

*1 quart*

*Britt Shockley*
*Broussard Catering*
*Lafayette, LA*

## BLUE CHEESE DRESSING

2 cups mayonnaise
½ pound blue cheese,
  crumbled
½ cup red wine vinegar

¾ teaspoon Worcestershire
½ cup sour cream
½ teaspoon hot sauce
½ cup buttermilk

Mix all ingredients, except cheese, with a whisk until smooth; add cheese and gently whisk. Refrigerate covered, for 24 hours for best flavor.

**Flavor of blue cheese can be adjusted by the amount put into the mixture.**

*Britt Shockley*
*Broussard Catering*
*Lafayette, LA*

## HERB VINAIGRETTE AND GREENS

4 teaspoons wine vinegar
1 teaspoon seasoned salt
3 teaspoons Dijon mustard
1 teaspoon pepper sauce
1 teaspoon garlic, minced
1 cup olive oil, extra virgin

3 teaspoons fresh basil,
  chopped
¼ teaspoon salt
assorted greens (spinach,
  endive, lettuce, etc.)

On medium speed mix all ingredients one minute, except olive oil and greens. Add olive oil slowly until all ingredients are well blended; pour over or mix well with cold crisp greens and serve.

***Keeps well in the refrigerator.***

*1½ cup*

*Patrick Mould, Owner, Chef*
*Cajun School of Cooking*
*Lafayette, LA*

# LOUISIANA CORN AND CRAB BISQUE

2 ounces unsalted butter
3½ cups heavy whipping cream
¼ large onion, chopped
¼ green bell pepper, chopped
1 tablespoon salt
1 rib celery, chopped
1 tablespoon hot sauce
1 tablespoon garlic, minced
8 ounces fresh cooked corn, reserving ½ cup stock
2 cups shrimp

½ cup dry white wine
1 pound lump crabmeat or 16 jumbo crab claws (optional)
1½ teaspoons fresh thyme
½ teaspoon dry thyme
3 tablespoons parsley, chopped
½ cup white roux (¼ cup oil and ½ cup flour)
3 tablespoons green onions, chopped

Heat oil and flour in skillet on medium for 3 minutes until blended; set aside. Heat butter in a 4 quart saucepan. Sauté onions, bell peppers, garlic and celery on medium heat until limp; about 1 minute. Add shrimp stock, white wine, thyme. Bring to a boil; add roux. Whip mixture to thicken. Add cream. Lower to simmer while whipping. Add seasoned salt, hot sauce, corn and corn stock. Simmer 3-4 minutes. Add lump crab, crab claws, parsley and green onions. Simmer until heated. Divide into 4 large bowls. Garnish with crab claws and serve.

*4 servings*

**This flavorful dish can well serve as the main entrée. Serve with Patrick's crisp green mix topped with his famous vinaigrette found in this section. Garlic French bread and white wine complete this wonderful menu.**

*Patrick Mould, Owner, Chef*
*Cajun School of Cooking*
*Lafayette, LA*

## SHRIMP iMONELLI

6 large shrimp, 6/10 count
1 teaspoon nutmeg, ground
1 tablespoon olive oil
1 teaspoon salt
¼ cup white wine
1 teaspoon black pepper
¼ cup heavy cream

1 teaspoon garlic, crushed
2 tablespoons fresh Parmesan cheese
1 teaspoon oregano, crushed
1 teaspoon black pepper, crushed

Place olive oil in skillet on medium heat, add shrimp, and sauté for about 4 minutes. Then add salt, garlic, oregano, black pepper, nutmeg and white wine. Bring to a boil for 2 minutes. Remove from heat; strain contents, holding liquid and removing shrimp. Put liquid in skillet; add cream and Parmesan cheese and bring to a boil. Add shrimp and let simmer for 5 minutes until thickened. Serve over pasta.

*2 servings*

**This recipe was a prize winner at Lafayette's Annual CFA, Acadiana Chapter, Culinary Classic.**

*Brian Blanchard, Owner, Chef*
*"iMonelli" Restaurant*
*Lafayette, LA*

# POLLO ALA GRANCHIO

**Stuffing:**

½ pound crawfish meat
1 tablespoon salt and
  pepper
½ pound shrimp 70/90
  count, peeled

1 tablespoon marjoram,
  crushed
1 tablespoon oregano,
  crushed
1 stick butter

Place crawfish, shrimp, Parmesan cheese, oregano, salt, pepper, marjoram, ½ cup Béchamel cream and ½ teaspoon garlic in bowl and mix.

**Béchamel Cream:**

1 stick butter
1 cup milk

1½ tablespoon flour

Melt 1 stick of butter in a 1 quart saucepan on medium heat; stir in 1½ tablespoons of flour until it is completely dispersed; about one minute; slowly stir in cup of lukewarm milk with a whisk. Whisk until smooth and creamy. Set aside.

**Chicken:**

5 8 ounce chicken breasts
1 teaspoon cracked black
  pepper
1 cup heavy cream

1 teaspoon garlic, crushed
¼ cup green onions
½ cup chicken stock

Pound chicken breast until ¼ inch thick, line with stuffing then roll, securing with toothpick. Melt 1 stick butter in a 2 quart skillet on medium heat; add chicken and sauté golden brown about 10 minutes; discard excess butter then add heavy cream, ½ teaspoon garlic, chicken stock, cracked pepper, green onions and ½ cup Béchamel cream. Simmer until sauce thickens.

*5 servings*

*This dish was a prize winner at the Acadiana Chapter Culinary Classic. Brian's mother is of Italian descent. He credits her with inspiring him to excel in extraordinary Italian cuisine with a Cajun flair.*

**Complete this dish by serving over pasta and complement with a green salad, English peas, garlic bread and white wine.**

*Brian Blanchard, Owner, Chef*
*"iMonelli" Restaurant*
*Lafayette, LA*

## KAHLÚA GRILLED SHRIMP PASTA

**Shrimp:**

4 pounds peeled shrimp, (10/15) count

2 large tomatoes divided into 6 even slices

**Marinade:**

2 cups Kahlúa
2 ounces hot pepper sauce
2 cups honey
2 tablespoons fresh basil, chopped
1½ cups salad oil
2 10 ounce bottles hot sauce
2 tablespoons fresh thyme, chopped

2 tablespoons Cajun seasoned salt
2 tablespoons fresh cilantro, chopped
2 tablespoons garlic, chopped
2 tablespoons parsley, chopped

**Pasta:**

2 tablespoons Worcestershire sauce
3 tablespoons red pepper, chopped

4 cups veal stock
1 pound angel hair pasta
corn starch to thicken

Mix all marinade ingredients; add shrimp and refrigerate for at least 6 hours. Grill shrimp and tomato over charcoal fire with mesquite and oak wood. Cook pasta according to package direction; in a 2 quart stock pot, reduce veal stock on medium heat for about 30 minutes. Dissolve 3 tablespoons of corn starch in ½ cup of warm water; use amount needed to thicken stock to obtain a creamy texture (covers back of a spoon). Add Worcestershire sauce, red pepper and pasta. Serve warm topped with grilled shrimp. Garnish with fresh cilantro and grilled tomato.

***This dish was a Gold Medal Winner in the 1988 Acadiana Culinary Classic.***

*Ken Veron, Owner, Chef*
*Café Vermilionville*
*Lafayette, LA*

# MICHAEL'S CRAWFISH CAPELLINI

1 pound crawfish tails
1 teaspoon Cajun seasoned
  salt
1 pound angel hair pasta
1 cup onions, diced
1 teaspoon Cajun hot sauce
½ cup bell pepper, diced

½ pound butter
1 teaspoon fennel seed
2 cups heavy cream
1 tablespoon fresh basil,
  chopped
1 cup fresh Parmesan
  cheese, grated

Prepare pasta according to directions on package. In large sauté pan, sauté onion, bell peppers, and fennel seeds, about 5 minutes on medium heat. Add butter, crawfish tails, seasoned salt, hot sauce, and cream. Reduce until sauce begins to thicken. Add pasta and 1 cup Parmesan cheese. Cook to desired consistency. Add more cream if thinner sauce is desired. Serve on warm plate, sprinkling grated Parmesan over the top. Can be garnished with fried soft shell crawfish.

*This dish goes well with a green salad, fresh buns and wine.*

*Michael Richard, Chef*
*Café Vermilionville*
*Lafayette, LA*

# ROULADES OF SALMON AND CRABMEAT

**1 pound salmon fillets,
sliced thin**

**Crab Stuffing:**

½ pound crabmeat
2 tablespoons fresh
Parmesan cheese, grated
1 stalk celery, chopped
½ bell pepper, chopped
1 pack filo dough
1 egg

1 teaspoon Cajun mixed
seasoning
3 tablespoons butter
1 egg, beaten for egg wash
1½ cup bread crumbs
½ cup green onions,
chopped

On medium heat sauté onion, celery, bell pepper and crabmeat in butter, about 10 minutes. Remove from fire and add seasoning and green onion. Add egg, bread crumbs and Parmesan cheese. Mix well. Set aside. Slice salmon very thin, about ⅛ inch thick, and pound lightly. Season with all Cajun mixed seasoning; brush egg wash on 4 sheets of filo dough and stack on top of each other; place crabmeat stuffing in center of the stack; wrap salmon around stuffing. Fold dough over top of fish/crab stuffing. Sealing all ends with egg wash. Place on a buttered pan and bake in a 380°F oven until golden brown, about 20 minutes. Remove from oven and cut with electric knife. Serve over Lemon Creole Sauce.

**Lemon Sauce:**

4 ounces dark roux
1 lemon, sliced
1 4 ounce can tomato paste
3 pints of shrimp or seafood
stock (or 4 seafood
bouillon cubes)
1 medium onion, chopped
fine

½ bell pepper, chopped fine
3 stalks celery, chopped
fine
2 tablespoons flour
1 tablespoon Cajun
seasoning, low salt variety
3 tablespoons butter

In a 2 quart skillet melt 3 tablespoons of butter on medium fire for 5 minutes. Add two tablespoons of flour and whisk until roux is dark brown. Add vegetables and sauté until clear; add tomato paste. Cook on medium fire until tomato paste is brown, about 10 minutes; stir to prevent burning. When sauce is brown, add seafood stock* and lemon. *If fish bouillon cubes are used, dissolve in 1 pint of hot water before adding to pot; add seasonings. Simmer, covered for 1 hour. Strain and serve.

*6 servings*

**This could be the main entrée preceded by Pat's Corn and Crab Bisque. Add wild rice, a cole slaw, and garlic French bread and wine for a heavenly treat!**

*Patrick Breaux, Chef*
*City Club of Lafayette*
*Lafayette, LA*

## LEROY'S STUFFED BAKED POTATO

5 large 50/70 count
  potatoes
4 tablespoons sour cream
½ pound cheddar cheese,
  shredded
10 slices American cheese
1 cup fresh parsley,
  chopped

5 ounces bacon bits
½ pound bacon, crisp and
  crumbled
1 bunch green onion tops,
  chopped fine
½ cup liquid margarine

Wrap potatoes in foil and bake in oven at 375°F until done; about 1 hour. Squeeze pulp gently, pressing through the foil; cut a slit lengthwise across the top; scrap out all of the pulp with a tablespoon, being careful not to break the potato jackets with mix; then cut potatoes in half lengthwise making 10 halves with foil still intact. Any extra potato mix can be distributed among the 10 halves. Top each half with a slice of American cheese and bake in oven at 350°F until cheese is toasted; if there is a delay in serving, top with cheese, cover tray with plastic wrap and refrigerate until ready to toast. If cheese is already toasted and refrigerated, remove foil and heat via microwave oven. Garnish with chopped parsley.

**Goes well with Leroy's brother's "Steak Morvant," a green salad, and garlic French bread.**

*Leroy Baptiste, Chef*
*Lebouef's Grocery Store*
*Lafayette, LA*

# PAT'S CORN AND CRAB BISQUE

3½ 1 pound cans whole kernel corn
1½ quarts chicken stock
1½ pounds lump crabmeat
1 teaspoon sweet basil
1 large onion, chopped fine
½ teaspoon red pepper
1 medium bell pepper, chopped fine

½ teaspoon black pepper fine
1 cup green onions
3 cloves garlic, chopped fine
¼ cup parsley
1 stick butter
1½ pint heavy whipping cream

Melt butter in 4 quart aluminum pot on medium heat; add onions, bell pepper and garlic; sauté until limp; add corn and seasonings; simmer for 10 minutes, covered, on low heat. Add chicken stock; bring to a boil; lower heat and simmer, covered, for 30 minutes. Adjust seasonings; thicken with amount of white roux (below) to obtain a creamy sauce. (Sauce will stick to back of a spoon). Cook for 15 minutes, covered. Add creamed green onions, parsley, and crab; simmer 15 minutes more, covered. Serve hot.

**Roux:**
3 tablespoons flour          4 tablespoons vegetable oil

Warm oil in a skillet on medium heat for 3 minutes. Add flour and whisk mixture for 10 minutes on low heat. Remove from stove and use to thicken sauce.

*4-6 servings*

***This would make a good first entrée in a seafood-oriented meal.***

*Patrick Breaux*
*City Club of Lafayette*
*Lafayette, LA*

## EMERY'S CRAB AU GRATIN

| | |
|---|---|
| 1 pound lump crabmeat | 1 pint heavy cream |
| 2 sticks celery, chopped fine | 2 teaspoons salt |
| ¼ pound butter | 1½ cups American cheese grated |
| 2 teaspoons flour | ½ teaspoon red pepper |

Melt butter in a 4 quart pot and sauté celery on medium heat until tender, about 10 minutes. Add flour and cook on low heat for 3 minutes; add cheese, retaining ½ cup. If too thick add two tablespoons or more milk; cook to creamy texture (will coat back of spoon). Add crab a piece at a time to break lumps. Turn off fire and place in 6 ramekins. Sprinkle top with ½ cup of grated American cheese. Bake in oven at 350°F for 3 minutes or until cheese is golden brown.

*Goes good with Brother's, "Leroy's Stuffed Potatoes," toasted garlic French bread, and an Italian salad and wine.*

*Emery Baptiste, Chef*
*Poor Boy Riverside Inn*
*Lafayette, LA*

## NOLTON'S CRAWFISH ÉTOUFFÉE

| | |
|---|---|
| 3 pounds of crawfish tails | 1 pint crawfish fat (optional) |
| ½ teaspoon kithcen bouquet browning and seasoning sauce | 1½ teaspoon salt |
| 1 large onion, chopped fine | 3 tablespoons flour |
| ½ pound butter | 1 level teaspoon red pepper |
| | 1 cup green onion tops |

Melt butter in a 6 quart stainless steel stock pot on medium heat; add flour and stir until roux is tan, about 10 minutes. Add onion and sauté until limp, about 5 minutes; adjust seasonings; add crawfish tails and simmer, cover for 15 minutes; remove from fire and add onion tops. Serve over steaming white rice.

*10 servings*

*Try this popular Cajun dish with fried shrimp, alligator, cole slaw, and "Emery's Crab Au Gratin."*

*Nolton Baptist, Chef*
*Poor Boy Riverside Inn*
*Lafayette, LA*

**239**

# GLOSSARY

*Allspice, ground*: Adds an aromatic flavor to certain desserts and a zesty flavor when sprinkled in water while poaching fish or making red seafood gravies.

*Basil*: A premier seasoning herb. Use it with seafood, meat, and dishes with wild game, including marinades, soups, sauces, stuffings, etc.

*Bay Leaf*: Adds subdued flavor to gumbos, gravies, and sauces.

*Bouquet Garni*: Consists of parsley, thyme, and bay leaf tied together and used mostly for gumbos, soups, and stews.

*Cayenne*: (Ground or dried whole). Cayenne is a calling card for both Cajun and Creoles dishes. Contrary to popular belief, good Cajun cooks use cayenne sparingly and only for its special pungent flavor—not to make food unbearably hot. Boil a whole dry pepper to have better control. (For example, two pods in three cups of water on simmer for two hours.) Add to dishes by teaspoonfuls to get the flavor desired.

*Cloves*: Like allspice, it should be used sparingly—about ⅛ teaspoon. Use in pies, cakes, plumb puddings, and other desserts.

*Celery Seed*: Excellent if used sparingly for fish stuffings and casseroles or in fish or meat dishes.

*Chili Powder*: Used in Mexican-related dishes and in barbecue sauces. (This powder is essentially a mixture of cloves, paprika, cumin, garlic, sugar, salt, and chili peppers.)

*Crab/Crawfish/Shrimp Boil*: This is the most commonly used blend of seasonings used in Louisiana to boil shrimp, crabs, and crawfish. (The blend includes mustard seed, peppercorn, dill seed, ginger, allspice, cloves, coriander seed, etc.) When boiling, fortify the mixture with garlic, onions, salt, and cayenne red pepper.

*Dill Weed*: Mostly used in poaching seafood or in salad dressings.

*Filé*: Gumbo filé is made from ground sassafras leaves. Use filé both as a thickener and for flavor. Excellent in seafood gumbos. Add to gumbo only after it has been served to individuals. Filé becomes stringy when re-heated. Old filé tastes bitter.

*Fennel Seed*: Definitely brings out Italian flavor in meat and seafood dishes, sausages, and pastas.

*Garlic*: This is a standard vegetable for all Cajun dishes. You can use garlic in many forms. Fresh is best, but powder and minced are popular, too.

*Ginger*: Used mostly where Eastern and Oriental influences dominate the recipe.

*Hot Sauces*: Basic ingredients used to spice many seafood and meat dishes.

*Lemon*: Use fresh lemon when possible. This is a must for most seafood dishes and Oriental and Eastern foods.

*Marjoram*: Has a flavor like a mild oregano, and like oregano is good in tomato-based gravies, rich cream sauces, or juicy casseroles with chicken, fish, or crabmeat.

*Mint Flakes*: Like lemon, mint flakes are excellent in melted butter for basting seafood like fillets of red snapper or flounder. Use also in tossed salads.

*Mushrooms*: Fresh or canned, these little morsels add the final touch to a deliciously flavored meal.

*Mustard Seed*: A standard ingredient for seasoning seafood. As prepared mustard, it is also used in marinades, barbecue, cream sauces, and gravies.

*Nutmeg*: Used in Oriental and Eastern-related foods. Nutmeg is used as a spice in sweets and to liven up crab cakes and fish patties.

*Pepper*: White and black pepper are made from the same pepper plant. (White is made by removing the black sheath of the peppercorn.) This is another base spice for most Cajun cooking. White pepper is usually used in light-colored dishes, while black is used in darker dishes. Black pepper is usually slightly more potent.

# GLOSSARY

*Rosemary*: Produces a mild, sweet flavor. Good for casseroles, baked seafoods, and in seafood stuffings. Rosemary is also good for lamb dishes.

*Sage*: Ground sage is best for dressings, stuffings. When melted in butter with basil, it makes a good basting sauce for baked or grilled fish. Use a dash at a time.

*Shallots*: Green onions with tops are a standard for most Cajun dishes, too.

*Thyme*: Thyme is a standard spice in seafood cooking. It is also used in stuffing, dressing, and sauces for meat and fish.

# INDEX

# INDEX

# INDEX

### Beaver Club of Lafayette
P. O. Box 2744
Lafayette, LA 70502

Please send ——— copy(ies) of *Cajun Men Cook* @ $ 16.95 each ———
Postage and handling @ $ 2.95 each ———
**TOTAL** ———

Name ————————————————————————

Address ————————————————————————

City ——————————————— State ——— Zip ———

*Make checks payable to Beaver Club of Lafayette.*

- - - - - - - - - - - - - - - - - - - - - - - - - -

### Beaver Club of Lafayette
P. O. Box 2744
Lafayette, LA 70502

Please send ——— copy(ies) of *Cajun Men Cook* @ $ 16.95 each ———
Postage and handling @ $ 2.95 each ———
**TOTAL** ———

Name ————————————————————————

Address ————————————————————————

City ——————————————— State ——— Zip ———

*Make checks payable to Beaver Club of Lafayette.*

- - - - - - - - - - - - - - - - - - - - - - - - - -

### Beaver Club of Lafayette
P. O. Box 2744
Lafayette, LA 70502

Please send ——— copy(ies) of *Cajun Men Cook* @ $ 16.95 each ———
Postage and handling @ $ 2.95 each ———
**TOTAL** ———

Name ————————————————————————

Address ————————————————————————

City ——————————————— State ——— Zip ———

*Make checks payable to Beaver Club of Lafayette.*